W0037926

"THE ENEMY WITHIN NEVER DID WITHOUT":

GERMAN AND JAPANESE PRISONERS OF WAR AT CAMP HUNTSVILLE, 1942-1945

EDITED BY
JEFFREY L. LITTLEJOHN
AND
CHARLES H. FORD

Texas Review Press
Huntsville, Texas

Copyright © 2015 by Jeffrey L. Littlejohn and Charles H. Ford

-

All rights reserved
Printed in the United States of America

FIRST EDITION

Requests for permission to acknowledge material from this work should be sent to:

Permissions
Texas Review Press
English Department
Sam Houston State University
Huntsville, TX 77341-2146

Cover Design: Nancy Parsons

Library of Congress Cataloging-in-Publication Data

"The enemy within never did without" : German and Japanese prisoners of war at Camp
Huntsville, 1942-1945 / edited by Jeffrey L. Littlejohn and Charles H. Ford. -- Edition:
first.
    pages cm
 ISBN 978-1-68003-028-0 (pbk. : alk. paper)
 1. Camp Huntsville (Prisoner of war camp)--History. 2. World War,
1939-1945--Prisoners and prisons, American. 3. Huntsville (Tex.)--History, Military--20th
century. I. Littlejohn, Jeffrey L., 1973- editor. II. Ford, Charles Howard, 1964- editor.
 D805.5.H86E54 2015
 940.54'72764169--dc23
                           2015003531

To Donna Coffen, James Patton, and the members of the Walker County Historical Commission for keeping this story alive.

INTRODUCTION AND ACKNOWLEDGEMENTS

When the United States entered World War II in December 1941, the nation began one of the most challenging periods in its history. Fighting on multiple fronts against Nazi Germany, Fascist Italy, and Imperial Japan required a massive military buildup and the mobilization of millions of troops. As American leaders struggled to construct a vast new war machine, they also had to prepare for the eventual surrender of thousands of enemy soldiers who would be housed in prisoner of war (POW) camps. By the end of the war, more than 370,000 German, 51,000 Italian, and 5,000 Japanese prisoners resided in 650 POW camps within the United States.[1]

This is the story of Camp Huntsville, one of the first and largest POW camps constructed in America during World War II. Located roughly eight miles east of Huntsville, Texas, in historic Walker County, Camp Huntsville was built in 1942 and opened for prisoners the following year. The camp served as a model site for POW installations across the country and set a high standard for the treatment of prisoners. Between 1943 and 1945, the camp housed roughly 4,700 German POWs and experienced tense relations between incarcerated Nazi and anti-Nazi factions. Then, during the final months of the war, the American military selected Camp Huntsville as the test site for its newly fashioned re-education program for Japanese POWs. During the fall of 1945, more than 100 Japanese prisoners took classes on the U.S. Constitution, civil liberties, and the nature of republican goverment, while they were incarcerated at Camp Huntsville. The irony of teaching foreign prisoners about democracy and voting rights was not lost on African Americans in East Texas who faced disenfranchisement and racial segregation. Nevertheless, the camp did inspire some Japanese prisoners to support democratization of their home country, when they returned to Japan after the war. Meanwhile, in this country, the U.S. government sold Camp Huntsville to Sam Houston State Teachers College in 1946, and the site served as the school's Country Campus through the mid-1950s.

This study of Camp Huntsville began at the urging of Donna Coffen, a local member of the Walker County Historical Commission whose mother, Nina Mickelwait Collier, served as a civilian processing assistant at the camp during the war. Donna suggested that the POW camp would be a compelling topic for publication, and she helped locate people and sources that were vital to the completion of this project. In fact, Donna's enthusiasm sparked Professor Jeffrey Littlejohn's decision to teach a spring 2012 graduate seminar on Camp Huntsville at Sam Houston State University. Students Micki Brady, Carolyn Carroll, Christopher Chance, Dan Cotchen, Patricia Hale, Amy Hyden, Natalie Miles, Sharla Morning, Bradley Trefz, and Dale Wagner all participated in the class. Professor Littlejohn would like to thank each of these students for their diligent work on this book, which is a testament to their efforts.

Earlier studies of Camp Huntsville proved particularly helpful as this project took shape. Frances Handley Bowers, the wife of former Sam Houston State University President Elliott T. Bowers, wrote a master's thesis on SHSU's Country Campus in 1950, highlighting its history and development. At the same time, reporters from the *Huntsville Item*, the *Houston Post*, and other newspapers wrote stories about the camp, and later local historians collected oral interviews for Walker County Stories and the HEARTS Veterans Museum. In addition, a robust literature highlighting the importance of World War II POW camps has emerged over the last four decades. Judith M. Gansberg's *Stalag U.S.A.: The Remarkable Story of German POWs in America* and Arnold Krammer's *Nazi Prisoners of War in America* appeared as the first works to examine the history and significance of the topic. More recently, Richard P. Walker's *Lone Star and the Swastika: Prisoners of War in Texas* and Michael Water's *Lone Star Stalag: German Prisoners of War at Camp Hearne* have highlighted the particular role that Texas camps played in the larger story. These books have been accompanied by an expanding literature on the treatment and re-education of prisoners during World War II. This project relied on Lewis H. Carlson's *We Were Each Other's Prisoners: An Oral History of World War II American and German Prisoners of War*, Ron Robin's *The Barbed-Wire College: Reeducating German POWs in the United States During World War II*, and Ulrich Straus's *The Anguish of Surrender: Japanese POWs of World War II*.[2]

In addition to these previous works, this study utilized a number of untapped archival and published sources to document the history of Camp Huntsville. The most significant collection of more than

550 pages of archival documents on the origins, development, and day-to-day operations at Camp Huntsville came from the Modern Military Records Branch of the National Archives in College Park, Maryland. To supplement this core set of data, we also relied on materials from the World War II Operational Documents Collection at the Combined Arms Research Library in Fort Leavenworth, Kansas. Additional local sources from the Special Collections Archive at Sam Houston State University proved essential, as did oral interviews with people who had first-hand knowledge of the camp, including Robert Anderson, Donna Coffen, Sam Dominey, Henrich Erichsen, Titus Fields, Nina Mickelwait Collier, Ray Warren, and Martha Wolfe. Finally, we discovered new accounts of the camp by prisoners who served time there during the war including Rudolf Thill's fascinating memoir, *Adrift in Stormy Times*, and the rare collection of edited lectures from the Japanese re-education program, titled *American Democracy and Its Ways*, by Moriji Yamaga.[3]

In undertaking a project such as this, historians incur many debts. We would like to thank our colleagues in the Sam Houston State University History Department—especially Thomas Cox, Brian Domitrovic, and Bernadette Pruitt—for their counsel, friendship, and support on this project. Edward Singer of Gallaudet University scanned and sent hundreds of pages of material from the National Archives in College Park, Maryland, to make this study possible, while Michael Waters of Texas A&M University offered keen insight into the story and wise counsel whenever we needed help. On the local front, James Patton, Paul Culp, Cheryl Spencer, and Barbara Kievit-Mason helped locate key documents and materials that made the story come alive. Finally, Charles Ford would like to thank Jeffrey Littlejohn for involving him in the project, while Professor Littlejohn would like to thank his parents, Ronnie and Patty, his wife, Mary, and his children, Greenley and Brant, for enduring much talk about POWs as this long-gestating project came to a conclusion.

Jeffrey L. Littlejohn
Charles H. Ford
12.3.2013

CONTENTS

Introduction and Acknowledgements   *i*

Chapter I. The Origins and Construction of Camp Huntsville   *1*
With Christopher Chance, Dale Wagner, and Carolyn Carroll

Chapter II. Early Life at Camp Huntsville   *19*
With Micki Brady, Dan Cotchen, and Carolyn Carroll

Chapter III. Nazi Prisoners and Problems at Camp Huntsville   *43*
With Bradley Trefz and Carolyn Carroll

Chapter IV. The Ethics of German Re-education   *59*
With Bradley Trefz, Carolyn Carroll, and Sharla Morning

Chapter V. Japanese Prisoners, Re-education,
    and the Closing of Camp Huntsville   *75*
With Natalie Miles and Patricia Hale

Chapter VI. Country Campus and the Post-War Era   *97*
With Carolyn Carroll and Amy Hyden

Appendix. The Geneva Convention of July 27, 1929
    Relative to the Treatment of Prisoners of War   *113*

Endnotes   *139*

"THE ENEMY WITHIN NEVER DID WITHOUT":
GERMAN AND JAPANESE
PRISONERS OF WAR
AT CAMP HUNTSVILLE,
1942-1945

CHAPTER I. THE ORIGINS AND CONSTRUCTION OF CAMP HUNTSVILLE

With Christopher Chance, Dale Wagner, and Carolyn Carroll

Huntsville Residents React to War

As World War II began in September 1939, Ross Woodall looked on in disbelief. After serving for a quarter-of-a-century as the editor of the *Huntsville Item*, Woodall had commented on many outrageous stories, but the brewing conflicts in Europe and Asia were among the most startling. Although the expansionist policies of Italy, Germany, and Japan were well-documented by 1939, Woodall could not believe that the leaders of those countries had already forgotten "the horrors of the last war." Indeed, Woodall noted in an *Item* editorial, the armistice ending World War I had been signed only twenty years earlier, and now, he feared, Benito Mussolini, Adolf Hitler, and the militarists in Japan were threatening to plunge the globe into another bloody conflict that promised to be even more deadly and destructive than the last.[1]

Nat Patton, Woodall's congressman from the Seventh Texas Congressional District, saw it as part of his job to keep American boys out of the impending world war. Between 1935 and 1937, Patton had voted with the vast majority of his fellow representatives in Washington D.C. to pass a series of Neutrality Acts, which prohibited Americans from traveling in a war zone, or selling, transporting, or loaning munitions or money to a belligerent power. These laws had allowed Americans to virtually ignore the military aggression perpetrated by Italy, Germany, and Japan during the mid-1930s. In fact, the United States did little to contain Benito Mussolini, the leader of Italy's National Fascist Party, as he established himself as dictator, launched an invasion of Ethiopia, and funneled arms to Francisco Franco and his fascist forces in the Spanish Civil War. Nor did the American government take any direct action against Adolf Hitler and his National Socialist (Nazi) forces when they won control of the German government, invaded and occupied Austria, and later demanded control of Czechoslovakia. President Franklin Roosevelt and the U.S. Congress also avoided any direct military action in response to the Japanese invasion of China and the resulting Rape of Nanking, opting instead to stay out of foreign entanglements as the militarists expanded their offensive posture. Indeed, in 1939, Patton voted with his like-minded colleagues in Congress to add a new "cash and carry" provision to America's Neutrality Acts, which allowed U.S. allies, Britain and France, to purchase war supplies and transport them on their own ships to the war zones. Such a move was crucial, Patton believed, because it would enable America's friends to fight the fascist forces then raging across the globe, while the United States remained isolated from the conflict.[2]

Despite Patton's support for arming the allies, many Huntsville residents took another view of the war. In early October, the owners of the local Avon Theater ran a half-page advertisement in the *Huntsville Item* offering free tickets to Adolf Hitler and Paul Joseph Goebbels should they want to see "All Quiet on the Western Front." After viewing the film, the advertisement suggested, Hitler and Goebbels would be "willing to admit that the world would be a lots (sic) better place" if they would "withdraw [their] troops from Poland and stop this Second World War."[3]

By 1940, the forced jocularity of the early war period had given way to a more serious tone in Huntsville. Local community members joined in a national drive to aid the people in Finland after the Nazi invasion there, and many residents felt a new sense of dread following the fall of France that June. In an *Item* editorial entitled the "Duties of Democracy," Hubert M. Harrison, the general manager of the East Texas Chamber of Commerce, argued that his organization and local chamber branches must encourage local residents to re-dedicate themselves to the responsibilities of citizenship. "In these ominous days," Harrison wrote, "patriotic businessmen must realize that a renewed idealism and devotion to our country is paramount to every commercial project. If our people cannot be awakened to a real and vital patriotic zeal for service to country, we may not have any business to defend." Indeed, the Chamber leader told his *Item* readers that, "We have been enjoying the RIGHTS of democracy and we have thought too little of the DUTIES of democracy. There can be no permanent rights under any government where the people do not attend to the duties of government."[4]

Stirred by the spirit to which Harrison had given voice, the Huntsville and Walker County Chamber of Commerce took action to meet both its patriotic duty and its business objective. On February 11, 1941, John T. Baldwin, the secretary of the local chamber, wrote to a hometown hero, Colonel John W. Thomason Jr. of the U.S. Marine Corps in Washington D.C., requesting aid in a local effort to secure an army camp for the area. Baldwin told Thomason that Huntsville and seven other East Texas towns were under consideration, and that local leaders believed their city offered the best location for the camp. "The citizenship is very enthusiastically in favor of the camp and doing everything in their power to get it," Baldwin told Thomason. "Anything you might do to help us present our claims to the authorities in Washington will be very much appreciated."[5]

As Thomason worked the back channels in the nation's capital, business officials in Huntsville hoped for the best. In a February 27 story on the local bid for a camp, the *Item* noted that Huntsville would become a "Boom Town" with 6,000 workers and 30,000 draftees should an army camp be approved for the area. Then, in August, the city's effort seemed to receive an added boost, when Huntsville hosted 5,000 troops at the Eastham Ranch with full community support. "These men, for the greater part, were draftees," the *Item* reported, "gathered from every state in the Union." The troops were well-behaved and orderly, and local citizens made them feel at home. "Should Huntsville be fortunate enough to secure an army training camp, this is the type of soldier that will become part of this community."[6]

The Provost Marshal General's Office Selects Huntsville for a Prisoner of War Camp

Although Huntsville's leaders never secured the army camp that they had so eagerly pursued, their efforts bore fruit in another arena. Following the Japanese attack on the U.S. Pacific Fleet at Pearl Harbor, Hawaii, and America's subsequent entry into World War II in December 1941, the U.S. Army Corps of Engineers issued a report on January 1, 1942, recommending that the nation's first permanent prisoner of war (POW) camp be constructed near Huntsville. The Army Corps explained its selection of the Huntsville site by pointing out several key factors that went into its decision. To begin with, the engineers cited the inexpensive and readily available land in East Texas and suggested that the relative remoteness of the Huntsville area would discourage escape attempts and prevent domestic acts of sabotage.

In addition, the engineers noted that the Huntsville site offered ready access to water, gas, and electrical services, as well as a state highway and a major railroad line. In short, Huntsville provided a perfect rural setting, far inland from the coast, and away from any strategic military installations.[7]

A few weeks after the Army Corps of Engineers issued its report, the Provost Marshal General's Office (PMGO), which had authority over all POW matters, prepared its own study on camp locations. Dated January 18, 1942, the PMGO's report noted the dire need for prisoner of war camps within the United States and recommended that two 3,000-man camps be immediately constructed, with one in Huntsville and another in Roswell, New Mexico. Following this proposal, the Army Corp of Engineers carried out a survey of Huntsville and the larger region on February 20 to determine the best location for the new

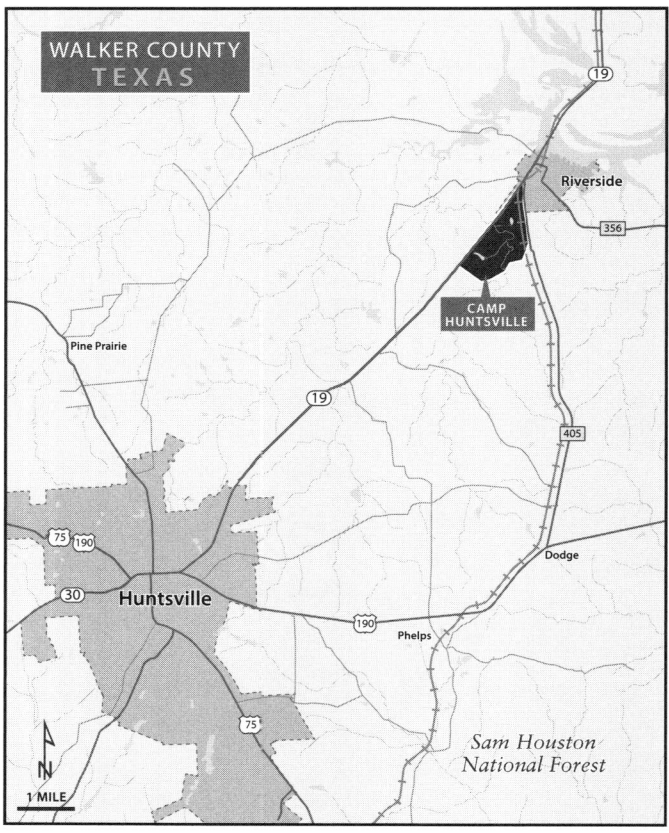

Map of the Camp Huntsville Site 1942.

camp. The engineers found a spot eight miles east of Huntsville to be ideal and recommended the purchase of 1,000 acres for the project, which it estimated would cost roughly $2.5 million. Four days later, the PMGO issued its approval of the recommendation, and on March 18, the Provost Marshal General directed his Chief of Engineers to initiate construction plans for the Huntsville camp.[8]

According to Frances Bowers, an early student of the Huntsville site, it fell to Colonel Nicholas Szilagyi, the Director of Operations and Training for the Eighth Service Command headquartered in Dallas, to acquire the land needed for Camp Huntsville. As an outsider who was unfamiliar with the area, Szilagyi worked closely with Gene Berry, a local lawyer and partner in the Walker County Abstract Company, who helped oversee the purchase of 807 acres from twenty-five separate land owners. Not all local residents wanted to sell their land, however. The Dominey family, who collectively owned several hundred acres identified for Camp Huntsville's construction, protested that their property was worth far more than the $25 per acre that the government offered. In fact, Maggie Dominey addressed a letter to Congressman Nat Patton, complaining about the situation, and he, in turn, wrote to the Provost Marshal General in an attempt to resolve the matter. This move failed, however, and, after several rounds in court the government agreed to pay Dominey $37.50 per acre.[9]

Once the location for Camp Huntsville had been approved, the PMGO's Chief of Engineers ordered that plans be drawn up for immediate construction at the site. On April 18, the Principal Engineer for the Southwestern Division of the War Department submitted plans for the camp and commenced acquisition of the necessary rights-of-way on the property. Then, on April 25, the PMGO approved the camp layout, and construction began on May 12.[10] Eventually, Camp Huntsville would serve as one of the military's six base camps in Texas that had been constructed solely to house POWs—the other five were in McLean, Mexia, Hearne, Hereford, and Brady. All other base camps in the state were housed on existing military facilities.[11]

In planning and constructing Camp Huntsville, the U.S. military took great pains to ensure that all aspects of the Geneva Convention of 1929 were followed. This international agreement had been designed to set standards for the treatment of prisoners of war, and some forty nations including the United States, Great Britain, France, Germany, Italy, and Japan had signed it by 1939. American officials hoped that if the U.S. military strictly followed the outline provided in the Geneva Convention in regards to the treatment of POWs, then the Axis powers of Germany and Japan would do the same with American

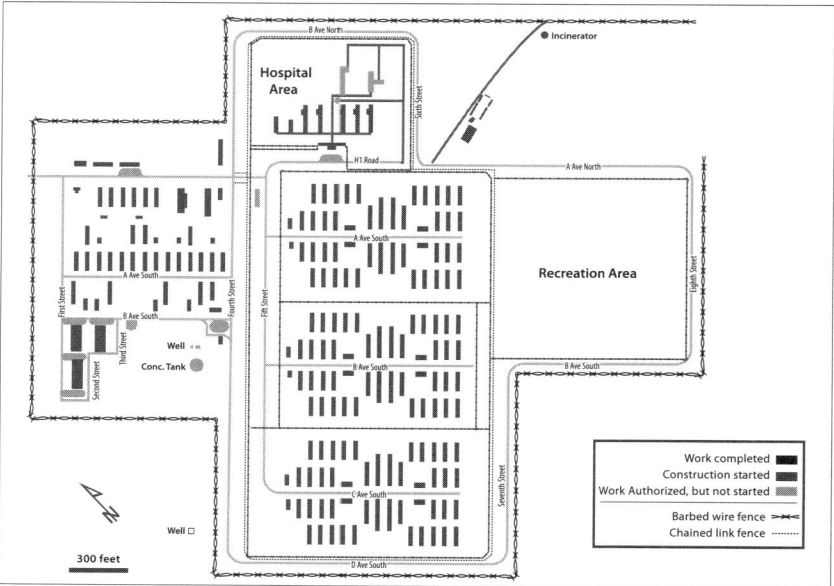

Map of Camp Huntsville, Field Progress Report, June 30, 1942.

POWs. The Geneva Convention required that POWs be taken to a location that was a safe distance from combat operations, and that they be provided with a warm, hygienic place to live. Prisoners were to receive medical treatment and the same amount of living space and food as the troops who were guarding them. The agreement also stipulated that each camp provide facilities that encouraged physical activity, libraries that encouraged intellectual curiosity, and a setting that enabled prisoners to pursue religious worship. Additionally, the Geneva Convention required the military to intern enemy troops in climates as close as possible to that from which they were captured. In each of these regards, Camp Huntsville proved to be a model site.[12]

Construction of Camp Huntsville

The Fretz Construction Company of Houston oversaw the fabrication and assembly of Camp Huntsville, which began in earnest in the summer of 1942. Located roughly eight miles east of Huntsville on Highway 45 (present-day Highway 19), the camp conformed in all respects to the standard design approved by the Army Corp

Looking Southwest at Compound #1 from 5th St. & H.I. Road; Fretz Construction Co., July 9, 1942. Courtesy, Sam Houston State University Archives.

Looking West towards the Post Exchange; Fretz Construction Co., July 9, 1942. Courtesy, Sam Houston State University Archives.

of Engineers. Only about 150 of the 807 acres purchased by the government were used for the buildings, sewage plant, and incinerator. A total of 405 buildings were constructed on the site, which consisted of four main compounds, hospital facilities, and recreation areas.[13]

The first three compounds at the site were designed to hold the POWs. Each prisoner compound included four sections of barracks, a shower building, canteen, mess hall, kitchen, and infirmary. The separate compounds were each designed to accommodate approximately 800 to 1,500 prisoners with tar paper barracks that were built for utility rather than comfort. The prisoners did have hot and cold running water, as well as a recreation room, and a canteen at which they could purchase special items.

Movement from the prisoner compounds into other regions of the camp was blocked by an extensive security system. Two ten-foot-tall barbed wire fences ran around each of the compounds and the recreation areas. Powerful lights were suspended from wooden posts placed at 150-foot intervals along the fence line, and guard towers stood outside the fence and offered American soldiers a birds-eye view of the camp and its perimeter.[14]

The fourth compound at the camp provided housing and administrative offices for U.S. personnel. Within this area, American servicemen had access to a laundry, bakery, barber shop, gymnasium, post-exchange, commissary, cafeteria, officers' mess hall, officers' club, and a fire station. American soldiers took advantage of these excellent facilities at Camp Huntsville, and the commanding officer enjoyed his own private residence near the entrance to the facility.

To the southeast of the American compound, engineers positioned the hospital complex, which served both U.S. servicemen and prisoners. In a 1943 evaluation of the camp, Dr. Rudolph Fischer representing the Legation of Switzerland and Charles C. Eberhardt from the U.S. State Department reported that Camp Huntsville had a "well equipped" and "up-to-date modern hospital with 210 beds and 7 wards." In the same report Fischer and Eberhardt noted that "the entire camp ha[d] been inoculated against typhoid, tetanus, and diphtheria." This attention to detail was an important part of the medical care offered at Huntsville and illustrated the excellent treatment that POWs received.[15]

Indeed, Camp Huntsville operated as a self-supporting city, with its own administrative personnel, police force, and local facilities. The site was so large, in fact, that the *Huntsville Item* reported in October 1943 that a "new town" named Carvolth had "been established in Walker County." Designated by the Missouri Pacific Company for its

The Main Transformer Bank; Fretz Construction Co., August 19, 1942. Courtesy, Sam Houston State University Archives.

Looking East from Central Ave. along the North Side of the Compound, August 19, 1942. Courtesy, Sam Houston State University Archives.

bus schedule between Huntsville and Trinity, the "new town" was actually the POW camp with a special name for the site's commanding officer at the time, Joseph R. Carvolth.[16]

Although the team from Fretz Construction Company worked quickly to complete Camp Huntsville, the project did not meet the initial August 1942 deadline. Nevertheless, with the bulk of the site ready for operations, Camp Commander Harry E. Fischer decided that it was important to go forward with a scheduled open house. He wanted to stress that there was nothing secretive about the camp. On September 18, 1942, hundreds of citizens from Huntsville and the surrounding area participated in a guided tour of the camp, which included a visit to the soldiers' barracks, mess hall and hospital complex. After the conclusion of the tour, the Walker County War Bond Committee chaired by Tom Ball sold war bonds and stamps to the crowd in amounts ranging from five to five hundred dollars. W. P. Mallery of Mallery and Smither purchased more bonds than any other visitor in a sign of patriotism that helped define the afternoon.[17]

After the open house festivities, an editorial appeared in the *Huntsville Item* welcoming the U.S. soldiers to the area. "Huntsville and Walker County has a reputation the length and breadth of this land as being a friendly place," the paper said, "and we sincerely hope that we will uphold this reputation by seeing that 'Our Boys' are taken care of in our homes, churches, places of business, and amusement centers . . . . Howdy Soldiers we're glad you're here." In fact, the local citizenry did much to support the troops during their stay in East Texas. For example, H.M. Stougaard of Stougaard's Nursery donated landscaping and plants to beautify the barren areas of the camp. "I offered the plants to the camp as a patriotic gesture," he said, "and as a contribution to the morale of the men."[18]

Revisions and Revelations: Changing Plans at Camp Huntsville

As the soldiers at Camp Huntsville settled into a routine, Lt. Col. Fischer resumed his focus on the camp's construction and development. In September 1942, he received notification that seven new buildings for painters, carpenters and utility workers had been approved for construction, as had stables for 30 animals, and nearly 1,500 feet of fencing. Then, in January 1943, the U.S. military issued several dramatic alterations to the plans for Camp Huntsville. First, the number of enlisted prisoners to be housed at the camp was increased from 3,500 to 4,800, and second, the site was to be further enlarged to accommodate a new 1,000-man compound for German officers. Both of these additions were significant. Under the existing rules, officers and enlisted prisoners could not be housed together and had to have their own separate facilities. Adding roughly 1,000 officers to the camp would mean that all of the existing plans for Camp Huntsville were now inadequate and would have to be revised.[19]

Estimating the accommodations needed for incoming enemy soldiers proved problematic for various reasons. The vast majority of the United States' early POW population came from the ranks of General Erwin Rommel's *Afrika Korps*. As the newly formed U.S. Prisoner of War Division found out, these men were not simply German Nazis. The ethnicities and political ideologies of the men in the *Afrika Korps* were as diverse and eclectic as the whole of Europe. The majority of soldiers captured in Africa were either German or Italian, but scattered among the ranks were soldiers of Polish, Hungarian, Serbian, French, Finnish, Belgian, Lithuanian, Estonian, and Ukrainian descent. U.S. Army officials learned quickly that, despite these men's willingness to fight together, their differences when away from the battlefield proved to be significant. Even amongst the German soldiers, political differences were substantial. Early on in the war, the U.S. Army made no distinction between Nazi and anti-Nazi German POWs. The failure to segregate prisoners based on their ideological feelings or national origins created a violent situation in many camps, where Nazis took control and dominated other POWs. In fact, as the U.S. Army began to recognize the diversity of its domestic POW population, the need became apparent for additional facilities to separate hostile factions from one another.[20]

Identifying the various ranks and types of enemy POWs proved to be very difficult, however. American GIs overseas were eager for German souvenirs. Guns, knives, and metals were all highly sought after memorabilia for American soldiers. Unfortunately for the men and women responsible for processing the flood of incoming enemy POWs, so too were military identification papers. The *Soldbuch*, meaning "soldiers book" in German, was standard issue for every German soldier. It contained such pertinent information as the soldier's weight, height, birth date, birthplace, parental information, and vaccinations, along with a photo and signature, as well as vital information regarding the soldier's military training, rank, and division. Those soldiers who did manage to reach the United States with papers intact, often made attempts to conceal their true identities from American authorities. The reason for this attempted deception was simple: the Geneva

The Sewage Disposal Plant—Looking Southeast, August 19, 1942. Courtesy, Sam Houston State University Archives.

The Incinerator—Looking Northeast; Fretz Construction Co., October 6, 1942. Courtesy, Sam Houston State University Archives.

Accords stated that commissioned officers could not be required to work during their internment, and non-commissioned officers could only be required to work in a supervisory role. As one might expect, many enlisted men tried to fool processing agents into believing they were officers to avoid manual labor.

The language barrier also proved to be a factor in the POW-processing effort. German-speaking American officials were few and far between in the early days of the war, and almost all of them were given important tasks in intelligence or overseas operations. Indeed, few were assigned to the comparatively trivial task of processing incoming enemy POWs. German soldiers could, therefore, simply pretend not to understand English directives, until they were waved through by frustrated American processors.[21]

As American officials attempted to comply with the rules governing the POW-processing effort, and new lessons were learned about identifying and segregating quarrelsome prisoners, the U.S. military began an extended, four-year program of building, demolishing, and reorganizing new and existing POW facilities. Camp Huntsville was profoundly affected by this process, since it was one of the first sites constructed in the United States. In fact, dozens of letters requesting changes to the original camp layout were written between Huntsville officials and the Provost Marshal General's Office in 1942 and 1943 alone. Among these letters were many minor requests to relocate various guardhouses, increase the size of the recreational area, and build a freezer to store the supply of rations. More importantly, however, there was also a series of letters dating from early 1943 in which the proposal for a 1,000-man officer compound was approved and cancelled five times by the PMGO, no doubt in response to the flood of German officers showing up stateside. On March 2, 1943, the PMGO finally decided that Camp Huntsville should not host an officer compound, due to the high number of enlisted men to be housed there, and it was placed elsewhere. Nevertheless, concerns over processing the POWs, segregating officers from enlisted men, and isolating difficult Nazi prisoners remained.[22]

Life before POWs

Shortly after construction began at Camp Huntsville, the War Department commenced with the staffing of the site. Captain George Leslie Smith of Rock Island, Illinois, and first Lieutenant Z.C. Rechel, of Fort Collins, Colorado, arrived before anyone else in late July 1942.

Both men were veterans of the First World War, Smith having served as a cavalry commander, and Rechel having served on active duty in France. These men had the responsibility for organizing Camp Huntsville's quartermaster branch. In the weeks that followed, a larger contingent made up of five active military personnel—two sergeants, one corporal, and two technicians—along with twelve civilian civil service employees reached the camp. Then, on August 15, 1942, the camp was officially activated and Lieutenant Colonel Harry E. Fischer, the camp's commanding officer, arrived in Huntsville with his wife. Colonel Fischer had served in the military since 1916 with appointments on the Mexican border, in the Panama Canal Zone, and in various spots around the United States. He was well-regarded by both his men and the local leadership, and he served in command at Camp Huntsville until April 1943. At that time, Fischer's hard work was rewarded with a transfer to the Madill Provisional Internment Camp Headquarters in Oklahoma, where he oversaw several POW camps in the southern section of that state.[23]

By October 1942, a large segment of the personnel assigned to Camp Huntsville had arrived, but important changes continued to occur. For instance, one of Commander Fischer's non-commissioned officers, Master Sergeant B.F. Krause, retired from the service, and the Army filled his position by making Teeny Halfant, the daughter of a Galveston businessman, the first woman in Army history to be promoted to Sergeant Major. The 20-year-old's duties at Camp Huntsville involved making out the daily orders and assigning both enlisted men and officers to their chores.[24] Civilian workers also served an important role in the operational structure at Camp Huntsville. One longtime employee at the site, Trinity resident Nina Mickelwait Collier, worked in the camp's POW processing division and struggled to identify and manage the paperwork for thousands of prisoners. Mixing civilian workers with military personnel at times became problematic, however, because the two groups did not always agree on how things should be done. One example involved civilian worker S.W. Lawless. Hired as a member of the fire department at Camp Huntsville, Lawless clashed frequently with military officers over procedures, and he became so disgruntled that he wrote to U. S. Senator Wilbert Lee "Pappy" O'Daniel to complain about military misconduct. Nothing came of the complaints, but they set a negative tone in the camp's fire department for several months.[25]

On a more positive note, in October 1942 the soldiers began a weekly news column in the *Huntsville Item* to create a sense of connection between the camp and the local citizenry. The first column, titled "He Wears A Pair of Khaki Pants," was written by none other than Allen Ludden, who later became famous for his postwar work as the host of the T.V. game show Password and his marriage to actress Betty White. The co-editor of the *Huntsville Item*, Nelda Woodall, agreed with Army personnel that the weekly camp column was a good idea, and she encouraged the soldiers to tell their stories. In fact, a young man named Gordon T. Miller wrote twice as many stories as Ludden did, and he oversaw the column as it changed titles to "See Here Private" and then to "News From the Camp." Articles by army personnel stopped appearing in the *Item* in mid-April 1943, coinciding with the arrival of the first German POWs and the naming of a new camp commander, Colonel Joseph R. Carvolth.[26]

In the period between October 1942 and the arrival of German POWs in April 1943, American servicemen as well as Huntsville civilians made use of the camp facilities. Young ladies from Huntsville's Sam Houston State Teachers College (SHSTC), chaperoned by civic

Personnel celebrate the opening of Camp Huntsville at the Plantation Club in Houston, Texas. Courtesy, Donna Coffen.

leaders such as Kate Barr Ross and Nelda Woodall, enjoyed weekly dances with enlisted men at the camp. Musicians from the Sam Houston College Orchestra joined with the camp's military musicians and provided entertainment for the dances. It turned out that even with proper chaperones, however, the love bug could not be stopped. By November 1942, the camp's first enlisted man, Sgt. Roy Schultz, married Huntsville resident Geraldine Davis. The ceremony was held at Huntsville's Memorial Hospital where Davis worked as a nurse. This was the first of many marriages between enlisted men and local women.[27]

Along with dances, stage shows and movies provided entertainment for the personnel at the camp. Traveling shows were provided by the United Service Organizations (USO), and the State Penitentiary arranged and presented one of its radio programs at the camp. Twenty Texas inmates under the direction of S.E. Barnett, the director of the prison radio show "Thirty Minutes Behind the Walls," entertained the officers at Camp Huntsville with a two-hour program of "musical numbers and black-face comedy skits." The first movie—"The Housekeeper's Daughter" starring Joan Bennett—was shown on January 8, 1943 at Camp Huntsville's own movie theater. Weekly movies began soon thereafter with titles including, "The Juke Girl," and "Sergeant York," along with military films such as "They Died With Their Boots On," "Dive Bomber," and "Captains of the Clouds." The State Penitentiary, Huntsville Chamber of Commerce, and SHSTC furnished the movies, supplies, and projectors. Colleges, including Northwestern University, also donated reels showing their football games.

On the parade grounds, baseball and softball were played with teams made up from the different companies. Other sports including basketball and soccer were also popular. Card games like bridge were available in the Service Club, and of course there were always things to do in town. The appropriately named Rev. Jimmie D. Troop served as camp chaplain and provided regular Sunday services, which were often attended by members of the First Baptist Church located nearby. Testaments for men of Jewish, Protestant, and Catholic faith were provided at the services. When not attending worship or participating in other activities, army personnel also had the option to enroll in college correspondence courses offered by the Army Institute and 76 participating colleges and universities.[28]

By April 1943, there were five companies of American service men at the camp, including three officers and 135 enlisted men. Life for the soldiers stationed in Huntsville was typical. They were expected to rise at sunrise and begin morning exercise, followed by breakfast. Whole companies at the camp rotated guard duty from day to day. Individual soldiers assigned to guard duty did so on a twenty-four hour rotation in which they were on duty for two hours and off for four hours. Officers at the camp were required to make an inspection twice during a twenty-four hour period, once before midnight and once after midnight. While on duty, guards were given general standing orders, with the harshest punishments reserved for soldiers found at their posts asleep or smoking. To prepare for the incoming German POWs, soldiers were trained to be on their guard at all times.[29]

Camp Huntsville was, thus, fully operational by the end of March 1943. It had taken roughly twelve months for the U.S. government to approve and purchase the site and for the Fretz Construction Company of Houston to complete the building process. During that time, American military personnel had arrived at the camp, a daily routine had been established, and positive relations with the local townspeople had developed. Throughout the entire planning and construction process, the U.S. government had emphasized strict adherence to the Geneva Convention of 1929. The stage was therefore set for the arrival of the first German POWs in April 1943.

CHAPTER II. EARLY LIFE AT CAMP HUNTSVILLE

With Micki Brady, Dan Cotchen, and Carolyn Carroll

POWs Arrive at Camp Huntsville

The first wave of German prisoners of war (POWs) arrived at Camp Huntsville on April 8, 1943. By that time, the European powers had been fighting for four years, and thousands of POWs faced the prospect of long-term imprisonments around the world. The first soldiers to enter Camp Huntsville came from Field Marshal Erwin Rommel's *Afrika Korps*, a German expeditionary force that fought in Libya and Tunisia. American forces brought the captured German troops across the Atlantic Ocean, through the port at New York, New York, or Norfolk, Virginia, and then by train to the small town of Riverside, Texas. After this extended trip, the Germans unloaded their gear and organized into groups for the three-mile march to Camp Huntsville.[1]

Some residents of Riverside recalled the first group of prisoners to arrive. The men were dirty, their clothes ragged, and most looked like they had not had a bath in some time. As soon as the "fall in" command was given, however, the prisoners began marching in perfect columns singing German military songs until they reached the camp. They marched swiftly, keeping their heads held high, showing how proud they were to be German soldiers. Considering their circumstances, the prisoners seemed to be in good spirits and had a positive attitude. One female resident of Riverside, Vernon Fitzgerald Schuder, age 27, looked past the poor condition of the POWs and saw big, blonde, handsome young men.[2]

The initial days at Camp Huntsville required quite an adjustment on the part of the prisoners. Once admitted to the camp, they were divided into 250-man companies and placed under the command of a German officer. Each soldier was then assigned to a barrack in one of three respective compounds, fed, showered, and issued a serial number for record keeping. Nina Mickelwait Collier, a civilian processing assistant at the camp, remembered that in the first few days after their arrival, the prisoners also received all of their basic inoculations, medical care, and oral interviews from camp officials.[3]

This process established a model that became the norm for many of the POW camps around the country. As German prisoners filled the camp, administrators and guards allowed the POWs to maintain discipline within the camp compounds, usually along their existing rank structure. Regulations specified that camps housing enlisted and non-commissioned officers would elect representatives at a camp and compound level; those elected, inevitably served as the senior members of the group. Among non-commissioned officers, those elected usually held a German rank that was equivalent to a U.S. First Sergeant. Among junior enlisted compounds, representatives were more freely chosen, but were typically the equivalent to a U.S. Corporal. While regulations expressly forbid these individuals, or any POW, from exercising any command or discipline function, in practice, compound commanders and guards worked through these individuals

Several thousand German and Italian troops being assembled in North Africa to trek to permanent prisoner camps, June 11, 1943. Courtesy, Associated Press.

A trainload of German prisoners passes through Tunisia enroute to prison camps. May 20, 1943. Courtesy, Associated Press.

and delegated authority in contravention of such rules. For the sake of efficiency, the lines of authority were often blurred. In fact, this arrangement made life easier for guards and camp administrators, and such procedures compensated for a guard force that was lacking in experience and manpower.[4]

Once the prisoners had grown accustomed to the camp, they began their daily responsibilities and settled into a routine. The morning began at 5:45 a.m. with the prisoners awakening to reveille, showering, shaving, and eating breakfast. By 7:00 a.m., most of the prisoners were engaged in some form of manual labor: mowing grass, repairing barracks, hauling supplies, or helping with food preparation. Prisoners ate lunch in their compounds at mid-day or took food with them to off-site jobs in agricultural or forestry work. By 4:00 p.m., most of the day's labor had been completed, and prisoners enjoyed games, music, and storytelling before dinner in the compounds. Then, it was back to the barracks for lights out at 10:00 p.m. As the POWs settled into their daily routines, they quickly learned the rules of the camp. Prisoners were required to salute American officers and follow basic military courtesy. They also had to stand at attention and face the music or colors whenever the national anthem was played. American officers did not have to come to attention to salute POW officers, but were expected to return the salute of the POWs.[5]

Despite the inherent tensions that existed at all POW installations, numerous sources demonstrate that German prisoners received excellent treatment while incarcerated at Camp Huntsville. Overall, the goal of the American military was to maintain order among the POWs by encouraging a positive outlook and disciplined behavior. This enlightened management was in sharp contrast to the treatment of allied prisoners in many parts of Europe and Asia. In fact, the American servicemen in Huntsville attempted to establish a mutual respect between the POWs and those in charge. As Lieutenant Joseph Suermann, the American company commander said at the time, "We have a tough job. And the best way to make it easier is to keep prisoners' morale high. We kid 'em along and they love it. You have to understand these men and get their confidence. Let them see that they are getting as good attention as our soldiers and they'll never give you any trouble."[6]

POWs Report on their Condition

Considering their circumstances, the POWs generally found their living conditions to be good. For instance, Oberschütze (Private First Class) Siebenbrot, a prisoner who arrived at Camp Huntsville on June 3, 1943, recalled that he found the camp to be clean and in good order. "Each prisoner was entitled to eat what a regular solider eats," Siebenbrot reported later. "We were given enough food, and there were few complaints." In addition, he said, "We were also allowed to learn several languages (English, French, and Spanish), and to read and write, and to study many different topics like math." Siebenbrot further remembered that there was "a monthly newspaper, put together by the prisoners," as well as "a chapel, an orchestra, a theater, and once a month there would be a big show, with the band playing, some would sing, and there would be a play or two." In all, he felt that the staff and soldiers at Camp Huntsville offered fair treatment to the POWs and did their best to make the experience bearable.[7]

Another prisoner at Huntsville, Obergefreiter (Corporal) Robert Ebinger, echoed Siebenbrot's comments in letters to Erna Meckler, a loved one at home in Heidelberg, Germany. In a note dated August 11, 1943, Ebinger reported that he was in good health. "I have gained weight compared to when I was in Africa," he said, "and my belly is bigger." Despite the "terrible heat," he said that he "still ha[d] a good appetite." Ebinger told his loved one not to worry about him. "In case of an illness there is a great hospital," he said, and the "medical attention is good and well thought out." In another letter dated April 28, 1944, Ebinger reported that he continued to be "very well and healthy." He had discovered that he could use his "trade in the camp," and that "once you get used to this empty place the activities allow you to spend the time well." Unfortunately, however, he said, "Sunday walks do not occur here, only walks along the barbed wire."[8]

Although the POWs faced an indeterminate period of incarceration, most of them found that their separation from loved ones was far more painful than anything that the American government did to them. For instance, Franz Büczolich, an Austrian POW captured fighting with the Nazis, wrote to his wife, Anni, in January 1944, encouraging the young woman to keep her spirits up in spite of his absence. "You don't have to worry about me," he said, "I am healthy and well." Büczolich reported that he had "spent the holidays in

New Nazi prisoners were fingerprinted and photographed on arrival at Camp Huntsville. Here is Tech. Sgt. Herman Moeller putting a 20-year-old *Afrika Korps* veteran through the processing mill. Courtesy, *Houston Chronicle.*

Nina Mickelwait of Trinity, stockade headquarters clerk, types up this prisoner's file, while Sergeant Herman Moeller keeps watch. Courtesy, *Houston Chronicle*.

satisfactory comfort considering my situation," but that his "thoughts [we]re always with you my dear friend and with our homeland." He assured his wife that he had "thought much of the good times" that they had "spent together in the snow covered Wienerwald (Vienna) Forest," and that he intended to return there with her in the future. For the time being, however, he reported that there was "no snow or ice" at Camp Huntsville. "It is a totally different world in which I live right now. The hours which I spend thinking about the past days are the nicest for me. I hope that this year a decision in the war will come, and I can be with you my beloved at home. Don't give up, I will be with you my love soon. I am not forgetting you and such days as we spent together are ever in my heart."[9]

Reflecting on his imprisonment years later, Martin Böning another POW from Camp Huntsville, said that he carried no bitterness towards Americans, but that the most difficult part of being incarcerated was the time he spent away from his family. "They treated us well," he recalled. "The camp was a good and clean place. I can't say they hurt us in any way. They didn't treat us badly . . . but we

Selected for labor on Walker County farms (with regular pay and an eight-hour day), these German prisoners chopped Texas cotton in blue denim garments prominently lettered P.W. Courtesy, *Houston Chronicle*.

were away from our families. My wife and I had only been together five days when I was captured."[10] The mental stress of incarceration and the feeling of isolation was common among the men, but the living conditions at Camp Huntsville seemed to have made a difficult situation somewhat easier for most of the POWs who lived there.

Nevertheless, one of the most common complaints among the POWs was that it took an average of six months to receive mail from their homeland. One of the prisoners from the *Afrika Korps* arrived at the camp on June 30, 1943 and received his first letter from Germany on June 1, 1944. Others, like Robert Ebinger, had to assure their loved ones that they were writing regularly. "When you are complaining about not receiving enough mail from me," Ebinger told Erna Meckler, "please understand that there is a delay. I always write my letters and cards." He simply wanted her to know that it took time for the notes to pass through the U.S. and German censors before it arrived at her door."[11]

Sometimes communication was so bad that no news arrived in Germany. For instance, one POW at Camp Huntsville, Johann Klassek, a veteran foot solider from World War I, who had been drafted back into the German Navy at the age of 49, was captured in 1944 by American troops in Cherbourg, France. His family in Germany received a telegram from German authorities that he was missing in action and had no idea he was held as a POW in Huntsville. Only upon his return to Germany at the war's end did his family learn his fate. Obviously, this situation took a great toll on his family, but Klassek told them that the people at Camp Huntsville had been humane and kind, and he assured them that he had received enough to eat. His only complaint was that he had experienced problems with his teeth, and instead of fixing them, the dentists at the camp pulled them and gave him poorly fitting dentures which made a clicking sound when he talked.[12]

POWs Enter the Labor Force

As the German POWs arrived at Camp Huntsville in 1943, farms and factories across the United States faced a critical labor shortage due to the draft. With millions of American men headed for the front lines in Europe and the Pacific, the War Department began to consider the use of POWs as domestic laborers. Although the protocols of the Geneva Convention exempted captured officers from forced labor, non-commissioned officers could be utilized in supervisory roles and enlisted men could be required to perform manual labor as long as they were paid and excused from war-related work. Some authorities feared that opening jobs to POWs might encourage escape attempts, thereby endangering the American people. The government eventually decided, however, to assign tens of thousands of prisoners to work as carpenters, field hands, custodians, auto mechanics, fruit pickers, and general laborers all over the country.[13]

In one of the earliest press reports on the utilization of POW labor, the *New York Times* featured three large photographs under the headline "German Prisoners of War: They March, Play and Work at a Huntsville, Texas Camp." This June 1943 photo-spread opened with an image of several dozen POWs in military formation, marching to a local farm with "shovels instead of guns." In a second photograph taken at the farm, the men wore shorts, long-sleeved shirts, and hats, as they chopped cotton under the "watchful eyes of armed guards." Finally, the third image in the set showed the POWs after a full day's work, enjoying "a game similar to soccer" in the warm Texas sun. Taken together, these photographs suggested that the American government had organized and employed German POWs in a useful manner, and that the men found their labor both difficult and rewarding.[14]

In return for their labor, POWs received special pay that could be spent at the canteen in their camp. All prisoners—whether they worked or not—received an allowance of 10 cents per day or $3.00 per month in canteen coupons. In addition, POWs who took jobs received 80 cents per day, half of which came in checks for the canteen and the rest of which was credited to their account book, which they could collect at the end of the war. Rudolf Thill, a prisoner at Camp Huntsville in 1943, remembered that the pay was quite an inducement to work. The canteen, or PX, had "shelves that were bursting with cigarettes, tobacco, candy bars, cookies, toiletries, and so on; and what with ice-cold soft drinks and with JAX Beer: all at rock-bottom prices."[15]

Initially, Thill found that "there were no jobs" at Camp Huntsville, "[at] least not for the latest arrivals . . . . What jobs there were had already been taken." Men toiled at all kind of work within the camp, cooking, cleaning, carrying supplies, and doing odd office jobs. Eventually, after several weeks at the camp, Thill finally ran across an advertisement for a position as an English-language translator, for which he quickly applied. After a short interview, he received a job making out the daily food requisitions for the POWs and American guards. He was the only POW in the office, and the Americans treated him well. He said that "they insisted he join them for the coffee breaks and for lunch. And, whether it was in the lounge or in the office, they never failed to act with something like good-natured equanimity toward him." Moreover, the job meant that he earned an additional twenty dollars a month, that he would be able to apply and improve his English, and that for the better part of the day he would be able to get away from the camp stockade.[16]

Although POWs toiled in a variety of positions, those in East Texas worked principally in the agricultural and forestry sectors. In a June 1943 article, *Business Week* showcased the Huntsville farm-work program and explained how it operated. First, local farmers such as W.L. Maxwell and H.V. Porter applied for POW labor and completed a lengthy approval process. Then, Huntsville Commander Joseph R. Carvolth established contracts with the farmers, specifying that they would pay the camp $1.50 per day, per worker. The prisoners received 80 cents per day for their labor, and the remaining 70 cents went to the camp for prisoner subsistence. As historian Arnold Krammer has shown, the "prisoners generally wore their *Afrika Korps* shorts and peaked caps" to work, "or in chilly weather, the regulation blue fatigues with the letters 'PW' stenciled in large white letters across their backs." Some landowners and field workers were initially weary of these new laborers due to the ratio of guards to prisoners. However, most of these feelings subsided over time. As *Business Week* noted, a group of "Negro laborers" in Huntsville "fled in fear at [the] first approach of the aliens with their armed guards," but were later "induced to return to the fields" and resume work nearby.[17]

In fact, field workers and property owners had a complicated relationship with the prisoners. Although fraternization of any kind was officially banned, it occurred on a regular basis. For instance, at the B.A. Eastham Farm, manager E.B. Fraser supervised the POWs in the fields, even giving instructions on the proper way to harvest the cotton crop, while at another local farm, Fred Dodge, Sr. oversaw POWs in his rice fields. Although these circumstances did occur, farmers were encouraged to tell the guards what work needed to be done, and the guards then gave the orders to the prisoners. In many cases, those prisoners who were able to speak English were made foreman over the field workers. One POW recalled that, since he could speak English, he was put in charge of supervising 10 to 20 men while working in the cotton and rice fields.[18]

Opinions concerning the use of POWs for labor were generally

A prisoner group is receiving work uniforms to wear outside the garrison. When these men received their denim, they had two uniforms each instead of only the shirt and shorts they wore when captured. Courtesy, *Houston Chronicle*.

German prisoners of war interned at Camp Huntsville left the stockade en route to trucks which took them to one of the farms they tended. June 15, 1943. Courtesy, Associated Press.

positive, and most American civilians found that the prisoners' "background of intense military training made them steady and uncomplaining workers."[19] Still, there was some grumbling. According to W.O. Simmons, a Walker County farmer, many local landowners requested POW help because they "couldn't get no other kind of damn labor." The German prisoners were good natured enough about field work, Simmons reported, but they "didn't know a stalk of cotton from a goddamn cocklebur."[20] In addition, a December 1943 report on Camp Huntsville by Rudolph Fischer of the Swiss Legation and Charles Eberhardt of the State Department noted that "there are many slackers among the workers" at Huntsville. In fact, Fischer and Eberhardt said, this was especially so "among those who are sent out to pick cotton. Most of them detest this labor. They rarely pick more than 30 lbs. of cotton a day when a negro woman or child averages 150-200 lbs. a day in the same area. There is evidence that a clique exists in the camp which induces many of the fellow prisoners to loaf on the job."[21]

Despite their relative ignorance about the East Texas cotton crop, German prisoners proved to be in high demand in the forestry sector. In fact, James Gilliam Gee, a Huntsville resident and professor at Sam Houston State Teachers College, serving during the war at Camp Gruber in Oklahoma, developed a plan to take German "prisoners of war out in . . . 'portable camps'" to do agricultural and forestry work. By creating small branch camps, Gee's program allowed POWs to travel outside the established base camps to do field work on-site for a number of days at a time. Gee received a military commendation for developing the project, and he later brought the "same idea" to the "East Texas lumber forests," when he served briefly at the headquarters of the Eighth Service Command in Dallas.[22]

Indeed, forestry officers visited Camp Huntsville, trained the POWs, and then helped coordinate Gee's program in which work details of eight to ten prisoners traveled with guards to cut trees in assigned areas.[23] Later, branch camps designed specifically for work details were created in East Texas by the Forestry Service and the Timber Salvage Corporation. Out of the twelve different

A group of German prisoners of war interned at Camp Huntsville tended local fields. June 15, 1943. Courtesy, Associated Press.

lumber camps that were created, three were managed through Camp Huntsville. These were located in Liberty, Orange, and China, Texas. From February to December 1944, more than 300 prisoners stayed at Camp Liberty in order to cut pulpwood. Camp China, though eventually used as a lumber camp, was originally developed for rice cultivation. Over 200 workers were sent to Camp China in 1944 to work in the rice fields. And, after the rice was in, the branch camp was used for lumber production until it was closed in December 1945.[24]

Beyond the timber industry, four farming branch camps administered through Camp Huntsville were developed in Navasota, Mont Belvieu, Kirbyville, and Anahuac. Prisoners in these camps helped farmers by clearing land, harvesting crops, and building fences, usually in a shorter, more temporary arrangement than in the timber camps. Around 100 prisoners traveled to Anahuac and Mont Belvieu for general agricultural labor in the fall of 1944, and around 200 prisoners moved to Navasota to help chop cotton in the summer of 1945. Camp Kirbyville, with about 150 prisoners, lasted only one month, while the men there assisted farmers in the area.[25]

Many of the POWs appear to have enjoyed working at the satellite camps because of the freedom and space they offered. For instance, on June 16, 1944, Klaūs Labeth wrote to his family in Dortmund, Germany, to tell them "something about our new station." As Labeth reported, his crew had been at a satellite camp for about four weeks. "In this new center," he said, "we are accommodated by

Two POWs from Camp Lufkin, Texas cut logs near Pollack for use as pulpwood. Courtesy, U.S. Army.

tents, which are occupied by six or seven men, which is better than the barracks, which are generally occupied by 40 men." He told his family that his tent was "nicely appointed" with "tables, chairs, and soon . . . a closet." In addition, he said, "Life here is a lot freer . . . . We have the tent open at night. To protect against the numberless mosquitoes we have nets. My legs are pretty much eaten up by the mosquitoes, but it won't get any worse and we have been inoculated against malaria."[26]

The prisoners of war also worked at the camp as carpenters, custodians, fruit pickers, office clerks, cooks, and commissary workers. Bess Woodall Murray, who managed the army and civilian commissary at Camp Huntsville, stated that the German prisoners working there were polite, well-mannered and creative. One POW in particular, nicknamed "Baby" because he was only fifteen years old, was mothered by the women who worked there. To show his appreciation for the good treatment he drew Murray a cartoon of the commissary with her in it. Murray went on to recall that there were more problems with the young American officers than the POWs. Many of the officers were fresh out of officer training school and were a bit arrogant and self-centered.[27]

Camp Huntsville Diet

The Geneva Convention placed very strict stipulations on the availability and quality of food served to the prisoners. Specifically, Article 11 directed that the food rations provided to the POWs must be equal to that supplied to American troops. To make certain that such provisions were carried out, inspection teams were assigned to report on the implementation of the Geneva Convention on a regular basis. The quantity of food served at meals never seemed to be in question during the first three years of the war. A POW from Camp Huntsville was quoted as saying, "On the first evening and on the first days, we were hungry, but we were soon provided with sufficient meals. We received good and adequate food. According to our orders to do damage to your enemy wherever you can, we naturally were always asking for everything we could get."[28] Titus Fields, who worked as a guard at Camp Huntsville, later recalled the high quality of the food service at the camp. "They ate exactly what we ate, only it was better. We had model prisoners, and they had the best to eat." Working prisoners were served 3 meals a day, an early morning breakfast at the compound, a prepared bagged lunch for their midday break during work detail, and dinner served upon their return from work in the evening.[29] Another former POW, Karl Heinz Blumenthal, spent time at Camp Huntsville and said that the "food was good, and it was plentiful. In both Hearne and Huntsville, the POWs had the same food as the GI's. I know this is true because later on I worked in the GI kitchen."[30]

The acquisition and delivery of food to the camp for prisoners and staff proved to be a considerable task. Many of the goods came into the camp from the train station in Riverside, Texas. Box cars filled with loads of rice, beans, potatoes and various dry goods circulated into the camp and were divided amongst the compounds. Necessary foods, such as cheese, butter, and meat went directly to cold storage units. Other goods were stored in the kitchens, many of which ran 24 hours a day. As Titus Fields later reported, "I have never seen so many potatoes in my life!"[31]

Careful attention was paid to the food preferences of native Germans and efforts were made to appeal to their tastes in order to reduce food waste. A POW Menu and Mess Guide was published in 1944 and catered to German prisoners' food preferences. The menu provided the POWs with various foods such as frankfurters, salami, bologna, cheese, potatoes, sauerkraut and bread. Cabbage was required to be served a minimum of three times per week. Foods that were unpopular, such as American style soups, frozen fruits and vegetables, and peanut butter were removed from the menu completely. The Germans also refused to eat corn, calling it "Swine Food." Former Huntsville resident Linda Evans recalled meeting two POWs from Camp Huntsville while visiting Germany in the 1970s. One of them, Herr Pfieffer, mentioned to her that his treatment at the camp was "OK," but some of the food was terrible. On Thanksgiving, the traditional American turkey dinner was served, and the prisoners were told that it was very good. Pfieffer said, in truth, to the Germans it was terrible, and they could not eat it.[32] Any dish containing oysters, celery, green peppers and canned juices were also removed from the menu because the Germans were said to be unfamiliar with these types of foods. To help reduce waste from the breakfast meal, bacon, eggs, ham, potatoes, and sausage were removed from the prisoners' diet and substituted with fruit, cereal, and bread because the Germans traditionally preferred a lighter breakfast. Beef was also to be served less frequently with a substitution of salt pork in its place. All of these efforts lead to a reduction in waste and aided many German POWs in adapting to their surroundings.[33]

Prisoners had their own cooks and mess sergeants, and the cooks prepared food in their own way. This well-equipped prisoner kitchen turned out some tasty dishes, American officers at the Huntsville camp said. Courtesy, *Houston Chronicle*.

Initially, the abundant amount of food served at Camp Huntsville proved to be popular with the German prisoners. This was the general case at many of the POW camps across the country. As the war continued, however, there was a six month period from mid-April to mid-August 1945, when a strict food rationing program was instituted due to a significant meat shortage in the United States. The severe diet restrictions were designed to eliminate waste and conserve food during the shortage. POW rations were directly affected by the reduction, which was to address the needs of the United States military and Allied Nations in Europe. These concerns caused a reduction in the amount of meats and eggs that were served at the camp and led to many complaints from the prisoners because they noticed a decline in the amount of food available. To combat the food shortage, prisoners were encouraged, and in some cases required, to grow their own produce. Persistent complaints from the prisoners located at many of the camps across the United States caused the reduction program to be abandoned by August 1945, just as the war came to a close. As the reduction program was lifted, an inspector from the Red Cross reported that the meals offered were of excellent quality and variety. He was quoted as saying "No one goes hungry among the prisoners at the main camp . . . All are very satisfied."[34]

Athletic Activities, Culture, and Academics

Prisoners at Camp Huntsville enjoyed a number of different recreational activities. The varied daily events served multiple purposes. To begin with, the activities helped assure that the camp met the terms of the Geneva Convention by treating the prisoners with hospitality and fairness. Frequent recreation also kept the prisoners occupied and happy, which helped keep morale high and confrontations low. Prisoners of war engaged in sporting competitions, classes in various disciplines, and a number of social clubs. Many of the men used the gymnasium for basketball and wrestling matches, and they participated in football, baseball, and soccer games on the recreation fields. German prisoners also made avid use of the prison library, garment facility, and bakery. They were provided with pool tables, ping pong tables, volleyballs and nets, and games such as backgammon, checkers, cards, bingo, and dominoes. Of course, additional gaming items could also be purchased at the canteen. Some of the men spent their free time playing horseshoes outside or sunbathing. Others used their time in the camp to build their own furniture and other woodworking projects. Commissary worker Bess Murray remembered that the POWs could take almost anything and make something out of it. For instance, the prisoners used discarded apple crates to make beautiful pieces of furniture. Charlie F. Parker, a civilian electrician at the camp, received a hand-made doll bed and wooden horse as a Christmas gift from the POWs.[35]

Prisoners also participated in cultural activities as well. Many joined in group choirs and orchestras. The men put on extravagant plays, complete with colorful sets created by the prisoners themselves. And, hundreds of German prisoners spent time throughout their days marching in formation and singing native songs together. While some men took the time in the camp to learn English, a great number of the prisoners sought education in other academic subjects. The prisoner roll contained a variety of doctors, professors, carpenters, and other specialized artisans. These men held classes on science, English, history, government, journalism, and even piano. The 'teachers' held discussions, gave exams, and even issued some certificates. However, not all of the learning that took place was just for fun. The War

Department and the Red Cross made it possible for the prisoners to obtain actual university credit for their schoolwork. Some men were even able to take courses from nearby colleges during their detainment. In order to facilitate this educational process, organizations such as the Red Cross helped to create a library for the camp. The library contained more than 2,000 newspapers, magazines, and books written in German. Guards censored the books, of course, but POWs also had access to phonographs, records, and radios too.[36]

In addition to the recreational activities at the camp, POWs also had the opportunity to participate in religious services. Although no U.S. army chaplain was assigned to the post during its early days, a pastor from Huntsville traveled to the camp to offer services on Sunday afternoons, and soon a Calvinist preacher from among the prisoners conducted services as well. At the end of the first year of operations at the camp, a December 1943 report by Rudolph Fischer of the Swiss legation and Charles Eberhard of the State Department found that the POWs were divided as to their religious beliefs. The report stated that "10% are Catholics, 10% are Protestants and the other 80% are 'Gottglaubens,' or believers in God but followers of no sect nor religious group." These figures may have disguised the true feelings at the camp, however, for by April 1944, a chapel had "been constructed by [the] prisoners of war from salvaged material in one of the recreational areas." The make-shift chapel sat 330 people, and army chaplain, First Lieutenant John G. Elser, of the Lutheran denomination, supervised the religious work of both the Calvinist preacher and a Catholic priest. In fact, by early 1945, a review of the camp found "a most encouraging growth of interest in attending church . . . in this camp above all others visited on this tour." Apparently 250 to 300 Protestants and the same number of Catholics were attending church every Sunday at Huntsville.[37]

Post Exchange, Mail Services, and Censorship

The Geneva Convention required in Article 12 that POWs have a fully furnished canteen where they could purchase a variety of toiletries, food, clothing and other necessities not otherwise available. At Camp Huntsville, prisoner purchases were made through the canteen, which was also called the Post Exchange, or more commonly identified as the PX. Products like tobacco, soap, toothpaste, candy, cold drinks and additional clothing were popular. Titus Fields recalled how the prisoners were also permitted to purchase one beer a week with the coupons that they earned on the work detail. John Warren Smith, a local 15-year-old boy who worked at the Huntsville PX, remembered serving the POWs alcohol. "There were three of us who worked each night behind the bar serving something like 2 percent beer to the soldiers." It was a job that no prisoner apparently wanted. "We simply kept on ice many cases of beer, uncapped the bottles for the soldiers and took their money. When they were finished, we took their bottles and cleared the tables."[38] Generally speaking, the prisoners seemed satisfied with the availability of goods for purchase at the canteens. In many cases, the POWs had more than enough money to buy the items they wanted. This issue became so common that the canteen officer at Camp Huntsville actually ordered additional items and leather goods—some that sold for up to $27.50—so that the prisoners could spend their money. In fact, Herr Schmidt, a POW that Huntsville resident Linda Evans met in Germany in the 1970s, still wore the watch he purchased at the local canteen. He said it was the best watch that he had ever owned.[39]

Though heavily censored, German prisoners were allowed to

German prisoners of war played Hundt Ball at Camp Huntsville, a game in which the players threw the ball instead of kicking it. Courtesy, Associated Press.

make contact and continue communication with family members living in Germany. POWs were given a two-part post card to write the names and addresses of their closest kin as well as their own return address on a detachable section. Upon successful delivery, the next of kin was allowed to return the detached card with an optional 25-word message to the prisoner. After initial contact was made, the prisoners were allowed to send two 9-line post cards each month to their nearest kin.[40] Workers at the camp processed the prisoners' information when they first came to Camp Huntsville and when they left. The information obtained upon arrival was used not only for administrative purposes, but also to help place the prisoners with certain jobs and living arrangements. For example, prisoners with a good working knowledge of the English language could be used as translators, just as men who had strong Nazi ties were housed separately from prisoners with democratic leanings. Workers also sorted the incoming mail before it was given to the POWs. Any mail that was deemed inappropriate or sensitive was held back. This was also the case for prisoner entertainment, books, newspapers, and radio.[41]

In February 1945, formal requests for a German-language radio broadcast were deemed unadvisable and consequently denied. An estimated 50 to 60 personal radios were used around the camp, though the stations were closely monitored. A field report in March 1945 noted that 60 to 70% of the prisoners made use of the library facilities. This large volume of participants made it imperative to closely monitor the books and newspapers being made available to the German POWs. Donated materials were carefully screened. Books bought in the canteen by the prisoners themselves were also censored, and any material that did not qualify for the approval stamp was removed. Both German and American newspapers were delivered to the camp, but only periodicals that met security standards were allowed.[42]

Conflicting Complaints about Camp Huntsville

As POW numbers around the United States grew in 1943, public attention began to focus on what some critics called the "indulgent" treatment of prisoners. Congressman Richard Harless of Arizona led the charge, alleging that the U.S. government was coddling Nazi prisoners, many of whom had engaged in acts of brutality against American forces before their capture. This opinion received eager support in Texas, where the *Fort Worth Star-Telegram* declared that even the Geneva Convention did not justify "pampering" prisoners or allowing them to enjoy "luxuries and privileges which are not a part of the soldier's regimen." Indeed, the paper said: "It is certain that if these camps were administered by former American prisoners in Germany, there would be no coddling of Nazis." The *San Antonio Express* agreed with this assessment. Noting that "German and Japanese [POWs] in American hands live far better than they ever lived before," the *Express* complained that "barbarian captors" in Germany and Japan "have made little (and in some cases no) attempt to provide their [American] prisoners with food, clothing and other care commensurate with those given their own troops." Reading such opinions, the American public questioned why—when thousands of American men were fighting and dying overseas—German POWs enjoyed grand meals, recreational activities, and a stocked PX.[43]

There seemed to be enough attention paid to the matter in spring 1945 to cause Dr. L.A. McGee, a professor of government at Sam Houston State Teachers College, to give a formal introduction to the Geneva Convention at both the local Kiwanis and the Rotary clubs in Huntsville. McGee briefly outlined the international situation and explained the reasoning behind American policies toward enemy POWs. Prisoners must be "humanely treated and protected against violence and insults," he said. In addition, "all houses must be sanitary, . . . the food must be equal in quantity and quality to that served to U.S. soldiers at the base, . . . [and] all precautions must be taken to maintain good health and excellent medical attention." These policies were not simply to ensure fair and equitable treatment of German and Japanese POWs, McGee told his audience, but they were designed in hopes that Germany and Japan would treat American POWs in a similar fashion.[44]

Despite the public's initial outrage at the coddling of prisoners, military planners believed that quality treatment of POWs was the best way to keep order in the camps. American officers supported the policies outlined in the Geneva Conventions and felt that prisoners who enjoyed high morale, suitable living conditions, and plenty of activity would not cause problems at the camp. This seems to have held true, for as the former German POW, Wilhelm Sauerbrei, who said, "If there is ever another war, get on the side that America ain't, then get captured by the Americans—you'll have it made."[45]

The high quality of living that the POWs enjoyed did not, however, please everyone at Camp Huntsville. In May 1945, an anonymous letter was sent by an American soldier stationed at the

Most of the prisoners were athletic, and inter-compound track meets, held at night under floodlights, were hotly contested. Here is another view of Hundt Ball, which was a favorite of the prisoners at Camp Huntsville. Courtesy, *Houston Chronicle.*

camp to Tom Pickett of the House of Representatives in Washington D.C. The letter complained of poor conditions and unfair treatment for American servicemen. The unknown writer, an overseas veteran, maintained that soldiers were required to work twenty-four-hour shifts, received minimal sleep, and were then ordered to complete menial tasks around the camp, while prisoners lived "in paradise . . . and laugh[ed] at us." Further allegations stated that Catholic soldiers were unable to properly observe their religious services. The letter was forwarded to the War Department for further investigation. Archer Lerch, the Provost Marshal General, replied to the accusations, stating that POW work obligations were much more strenuous than the critic implied. He refuted the other accusations as well, arguing that the prisoners were in no way living "in paradise," and that they did not receive any benefits their American guards did not enjoy.[46] In fact, Lerch might have pointed out that American servicemen lived in a positive environment at Camp Hutnsville and had plenty of recreation

Prisoners at Camp Huntsville formed musical and theater groups for entertainment. Courtesy, *Houston Chronicle*.

time when not on duty. There were even dances held once monthly at the recreation hall with buses of girls brought in by the local United Service Organization (U.S.O.).[47]

Escape Attempts and Punishment

Escape attempts at Camp Huntsville were infrequent and largely unsuccessful. This was due primarily to the location of the camp. Even if prisoners could escape the compound, they soon found themselves in the middle of a rural farming area with few viable options. Once the alarm sounded to signal an escape, the guards sent out bloodhounds to hunt down the prisoners. Typical was the case of Edwin G. Kluckman, a 26-year-old German prisoner at Huntsville, who was recaptured in less than 12 hours only a mile from camp. More ominous was the case of prisoner Josef Wintzen who disappeared from camp on April 8, 1944, after receiving distressing news in the mail concerning his family back home. Investigators found his body on April 19, hung in the woods outside the camp. The POWs sometimes attributed such cases to guards carrying out illegal justice, though in this case it was ruled a suicide. These and a few other minor escape attempts occurred at Camp Huntsville, but all were quickly resolved, and the prisoners returned. Punishment for escape usually meant confinement in the stockade for 30 days as long as a prisoner had not stolen anything. According to the Geneva Convention, theft by a POW, like sabotage and murder, was a criminal offense punishable under the laws of the host nation; in the United States, that meant a military court-martial. That said, the general rule of "no harm, no foul" applied to escape attempts, whereas criminal activity was a different matter. Texas saw few escape attempts compared to other states with smaller prisoner populations, and Huntsville saw fewer than most other camps.[48]

During the entire course of the war, the FBI and local authorities captured all but 24 of the 2,802 POWs who escaped prison facilities across the U.S. The majority of the fugitives were caught within a day or two of their escape. Only one prisoner made it all the way to Germany and returned to the fight during the war. Meanwhile, another POW, Georg Gaertner, escaped from a camp in New Mexico and managed to remain free until the 1990s. After turning himself into authorities, the U.S. allowed him to remain.[49]

Given the few escape attempts at Camp Huntsville, some POWs worked on farms without guards by 1945. Despite the opportunity that this represented for escape, few prisoners were motivated to take it, and those who did seemed to have done it out of a sense of adventure rather than of nefarious intent. In fact, the POW system had a better escape record than the federal penitentiary system, where prisoners were more heavily guarded and secured. More significantly, beyond the occasional work slowdown or stoppage, there seem to have been few attempts by fugitives to commit sabotage or other troublemaking. Nevertheless, as the following chapter shows, there were significant problems within Camp Huntsville and other sites that demanded swift and stern discipline.[50]

CHAPTER III. NAZI PRISONERS AND PROBLEMS AT CAMP HUNTSVILLE

With Bradley Trefz and Carolyn Carroll

Nazi Problems Emerge at Camp Huntsville

By late summer 1943, American guards at Camp Huntsville had grown accustomed to the workday routine. During time on-duty, guards kept watch in the towers, and the men protecting the compounds rotated positions regularly. To keep order in the camp, one man served as the senior officer during each shift, and the guards conducted mandatory inspections of all prisoner compounds. The lead officer of the day was required to oversee an inspection of each compound every twelve hours. In addition, the guards at Camp Huntsville had strict orders to follow; men's lockers and personal effects were to be kept in pristine order, and they were not allowed to sleep or smoke while on duty. The general orders required each man "to take charge of his post and all government property. To walk his post in a military manner, keeping always on the alert, observing everything that takes place within sight or hearing."[1] Furthermore, camp commanders and their staff were subject to repeat inspections. Officials from the Provost Marshal General's Office, State Department, Swiss Legation, Red Cross, and YMCA visited regularly to assess the camp, its operations, and the condition of the prisoners.

As a result of these continuing inspections, the Provost Marshal General's Office became aware of an emerging problem at Camp Huntsville and other sites around the nation in 1943. Put simply, Nazi soldiers were beating, intimidating, and demanding deference from anti-Nazi soldiers who had been captured with them. In response to this developing issue, officials began a belated classification and segregation program that attempted to separate trouble-makers, including Nazi hardliners, members of the *Schutzstaffel* (SS), and Gestapo agents, as well as anti-Nazi agitators, from other prisoners.

Special "Nazi" and "anti-Nazi" camps reserved for the most difficult and disruptive prisoners were established. At Camp Huntsville, the commanding officer, Colonel Joseph R. Carvolth, began transferring some of his most disruptive prisoners to the new hardline camps in the summer of 1943. Since he was primarily concerned with discipline and order, Carvolth ironically decided to send the anti-Nazis away first, since they were generally in the minority and requested transfers themselves. By mid-July 1943, Camp Huntsville had requested to send 51 anti-Nazis to one of the Army's new anti-Nazi sites, Camp McCain, Mississippi. Then, on September 14, Carvolth identified 37 prisoners as "Nazi leaders, extremists and chronic trouble makers" and sent them to Camp Alva, Oklahoma, the newly designated "Nazi" camp for hard cases.[2]

Despite these transfers, the new program for troublesome POWs did not work entirely as intended. Since the U.S. military failed to establish clear guidelines for determining which prisoners should be transferred, the decision was left completely to local commanders. An "ardent Nazi" to one U.S. commander, might be a model prisoner to another. Colonel Carvolth thus found himself on the receiving end of the prison transfer system, with hardened Nazis and other problem prisoners sent to him from camps Hearne and Brady in Texas, and Camp Tonkawa in Oklahoma. As those camps filled with non-commissioned officers, their overflow ended up at Camp Huntsville, which had primarily held lower-level enlisted prisoners through the fall of 1943. It appears that the "overflow" often consisted of troublesome cases, as camp commanders passed their problems down the line in time-honored bureaucratic fashion. Making matters worse, Camp Huntsville still contained a population of ardent anti-Nazis in late 1943, despite earlier outbound transfers to Camp McCain. Given such a volatile mix, attempts to control the camp proved to be difficult. In fact, reports of late night beatings and threats of murder ran through the camp.[3]

Indeed, as anti-Nazi numbers at Camp Huntsville declined, the majority of the remaining prisoners supported and emboldened the Nazi elements. And, thus, transfers proved only marginally effective. As quickly as Nazis were transferred from the camp in 1943 and 1944, more arrived from other camps, including a large number of SS and Gestapo men, leading to one 1945 report that described Huntsville as "a dumping ground for incorrigible Nazis."[4] Partly this was due to the nature of the POW labor program. Over time, many junior enlisted prisoners at Camp Huntsville moved to various work camps, and the empty space they left at the Huntsville base camp filled with

A guard keeping watch at Camp Huntsville. Courtesy, *Houston Chronicle*.

non-commissioned officers, who, under the Geneva Convention, did not have to work. These non-commissioned officers tended to be Nazis who were more political than the junior enlisted men they replaced; in addition, they often received the much-coveted authority delegated by American officers to senior POWs. These hardline elements quickly extended complete internal control over the camp and used violence, intimidation, and threats to exert their authority over the German prisoners.[5]

Nazi control over the POW mail system at nearby Camp Hearne, Texas, partly facilitated Nazi control at Huntsville, by allowing the Nazis to communicate between camps and identify transferred anti-Nazis. Thus, in addition to the constant transfer of personnel, the mail system allowed Nazi elements to coordinate actions against their targets beyond the confines of their immediate camps. A German plan further aided inter-camp communication. Discovered by American intelligence in 1943, the Germans had made provisions to include Gestapo agents amongst Germans captured during the war, with special training on methods of clandestine communication, both between camps, and back to Germany.[6]

German versus German

Interestingly, in 1943, administrators at Camp Huntsville and the Eighth Service Command seem to have been primarily concerned with ridding the camps of the anti-Nazis who were viewed as a "potential source of disturbance" and "trouble-makers,"[7] rather than the die-hard Nazis. Yet, the problems at Camp Huntsville and other sites ran deeper than a few outspoken anti-Nazis. The reasons for Huntsville's continued problems dated to its inception. The majority of the men at the camp were from the *Afrika Korps* captured during operations early in the war. Unlike many of the prisoners captured in Italy and Europe, who would later populate the camp, these men were part of the professional German Army, and included a significant proportion of political Nazis, SS, and Gestapo men. The United States, despite admonishment from the more experienced British, had failed to screen the majority of its POW population. As a result, a minority of anti-Nazis mixed with this much larger general population of prisoners. That minority would come under regular

These barbed-wire fences surrounded the prison and separated the compounds. In towers, spaced at intervals, guards watched over the POWs. Courtesy, *Houston Chronicle*.

attack throughout the war, but Huntsville was an especially bad place to be an anti-Nazi.[8]

The anti-Nazis did little to help their own cause with the Americans, however. Many were radicals who were aligned with left-wing elements that had been suppressed in Germany in 1919 by returning members of the army after the November 11 Armistice. Others were former political prisoners with communist leanings or avowed members of the communist party. Their radicalism sometimes led to counter-productive behavior, like refusals to salute American officers as part of a general rejection of militarism and not just Nazism. In contrast, Nazis appear to have relished delivering their stiff armed salute to the Americans. Both the refusal to salute and the Nazi salute were essentially political acts, but the Nazi salute, in context, was a proper rendering of military courtesy, whereas the Americans viewed the refusal to salute as subversive and unbecoming of a military member.[9]

Anti-Nazis also considered themselves "free" of past constraints; *Freiheit hinter Staacheldraht* (freedom behind barbed wire) as they called it. This led to outspoken behavior in which they freely discussed the downfall of the Hitler regime and preached their political beliefs. They also considered the Americans allies and wanted to help them, which they usually did by informing on their fellow prisoners. Consequently, their fellow prisoners, even those who were not ardent Nazis, viewed anti-Nazis as traitors, deserters, and snitches, and they were a constant source of trouble within camps where their numbers offered them a degree of safety.[10]

It should not be surprising, then, that American guards generally viewed the anti-Nazis through a similar lens as the Nazis—many of the anti-Nazis *were* traitors and snitches to their own side, and generally disruptive in many cases. Anti-Nazis, like defectors, spies, or snitches, were greeted with suspicion and a certain amount of distaste, even when they provided valuable information. However noble their motives, the consequence of their actions meant their captors often treated anti-Nazis with a degree of suspicion.

In any case, camp administrators were more concerned with order and discipline within their camps than with any political argument between Germans, who were, as a group, viewed as the "enemy." Any anti-Nazi attempting to cozy up to guards, demanding special treatment, or causing trouble, was a problem, no matter the political reasoning behind it. Until the development of the re-education program later in the war, which channeled the activities of the anti-Nazis into a U.S. coordinated program, the activities of most anti-

Nazis within their respective camps caused problems and garnered few converts to their cause.

Penal Battalions and Foreign Soldiers

At the height of the 1943 Nazi- and anti-Nazi crisis, Camp Huntsville proved to be a particularly important spot within the national POW system. At Huntsville, the general population of *Afrika Korps* non-commissioned officers (NCOs) and enlisted men were mixed with political prisoners, criminals, and anti-Nazis. Some of these prisoners likely came from the 999th Light *Afrika* Division, which contained the majority of anti-Nazis captured early in the war. Originally created as a penal brigade in 1942 in France, the unit expanded into a Division and began deployment into North Africa in early 1943. The defeat of German forces in North Africa interrupted the deployment, however, and many of the unit's members quickly surrendered without a fight to the first Americans they encountered. Such actions did not endear them to their fellow POWs who viewed them as deserters and traitors. Despite the obvious divisions between these German prisoners, the POW camps in North Africa did not attempt to organize the prisoners, but rather mixed them all together in large compounds. This led to a number of problems with identification and organization. It also meant that the prisoners from the 999th were scattered throughout the early POW population and camp system.[11]

The enlisted members of the unit were primarily communists, traditional socialists, anti-Nazis, and criminals, while their non-commissioned officers and officers were trusted party men. Just as the non-commissioned officers of the *Afrika Korps* tended to be the most ardent Nazis, the enlisted men of the 999th tended to be the most radical anti-Nazis. Much of the 999th's more senior non-commissioned officers and leadership were confirmed Nazis and included Gestapo men, who were put in place to "keep watch" over their radical troops. Thus, the stage was set for violence whenever these two forces found themselves occupying the same camp in significant numbers.[12]

In his account of his time at Camp Huntsville, former POW Rudolf Thill identifies twelve of the anti-Nazis who arrived with him as part of the first batch of prisoners who had been released from concentration camps to serve in the penal battalions of units like the 999th. These men had a particular problem in that their arms bore the telltale number tattoos of concentration camp prisoners. This made it nearly impossible for them to blend in with the prisoner population, even if they wanted to, which by all appearances they did not. Eventually, following an attack on two prisoners, the twelve anti-Nazis along with Thill, who had taken a job working with the Americans, were transferred to another camp after being segregated from the other prisoners and placed in the stockade for their own protection. More transfers and violence would follow.[13]

In fact, disagreements among the "German" soldiers proved to be the greatest disruptive force at Camp Huntsville. This was, in large part, because the German military was not nearly as homogenous as it has often been portrayed. In addition to a large number of Austrians pressed into service, it included Poles, Ukrainians, Russians, Lithuanians, and any number of Balkan partisans who found themselves serving in the *Wehrmacht* or in specially organized foreign units. The U.S. generally treated all of these men as "German" on the basis that they were captured in German uniform, at least until later in the war.

Hans Wilfanger, an Austrian pressed into the German Army, served as one such prisoner. An anti-Nazi, he had briefly worked for the British after being captured before his transfer into American custody. When he arrived at Camp Huntsville, word spread of his

The Sentry Towers, Floodlighting and Fencing at Camp Huntsville. Courtesy, Sam Houston State University Archives.

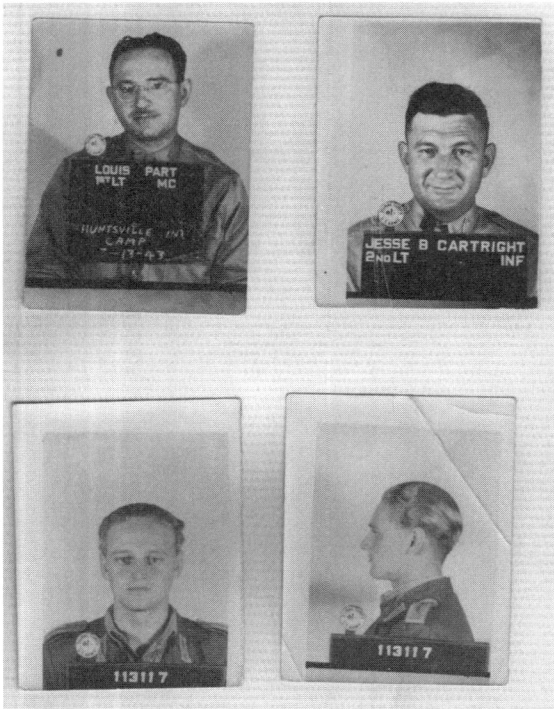

Individual soldiers at Camp Huntsville, from Nina Mickelwait's scrapbook. Courtesy, Donna Coffen.

affiliation, and it was not long before he was attacked by a group of ardent Nazis in early 1944. Despite an extended period of hospitalization, and the inability to identify his attackers, he gave the camp intelligence officer vital information regarding the Nazi and SS membership within the camp.[14]

Fortunately for camp administrators, it appears that no prisoners of Russian/ Soviet origin remained in Huntsville by late 1943. In addition to issues like those experienced by Wilfanger, distrust by the Germans, and the language barrier, these prisoners sometimes resisted their repatriation at war's end. In one of the final atrocities of the war, under the terms of a secret agreement arranged at the Yalta conference, the U.S. and Great Britain repatriated those POWs of Soviet origin who had fought with the Germans to the Soviet Union. Stalin ordered the execution of thousands of such prisoners as traitors, with the rest sent to the Soviet gulags to die.

The Riot: November 25, 1943

Despite all the internal turmoil at Camp Huntsville, Nazi actions largely remained covert, while anti-Nazi actions were more visible. Violence against anti-Nazis often took the form of attacks in the barracks at night. During the day, anti-Nazis were shunned and ostracized, and frequent targets of insult and derogatory remarks. On

Nazi soldiers from the *Afrika Korps* at nearby Camp Hearne. Courtesy, Friends of Camp Hearne.

occasion, however, the level of violence became so great that guards had to intervene. In November 1943, Camp Huntsville had a major riot, which in combination with events occurring elsewhere, led to significant changes in POW administration throughout 1944.

Around eight o'clock on the evening of November 25, 1943, events at Camp Huntsville began to unfold. Senior non-commissioned officers and Nazi hardliners, after several days of increasing tension with anti-Nazi prisoners, launched an orgy of violence. After arming themselves with clubs, the Nazis attacked the anti-Nazis on one of the streets of the compound. The Nazis carried out a carefully planned and coordinated attack that resulted in a number of anti-Nazis receiving beatings so severe that they required hospitalization and were left near dead.[15]

Guards struggled to respond to and put down the violence, but Nazi sympathizers physically blocked their entry to the scene of the conflict, forming a large crowd that refused to disperse. Fighting their way through the human blockade with clubs and fists, the guards finally broke into the area. One of the perpetrators immediately broke

The POW Post Office at Camp Hearne, which oversaw the mail system for all prisoner of war camps in the U.S. Courtesy, Friends of Camp Hearne.

for the fence line. Ordered to halt three times, he refused to comply. The sole fatality of the night occurred when a guard shot and killed the Nazi perpetrator as he approached the fence.[16]

The second shooting of the evening took place when an officer of the guard force entered a latrine in pursuit of a fleeing Nazi. Unbeknownst to him, one of the Nazis armed with a large club lay in wait for him outside. An armed guard, seeing the hiding prisoner, ordered him to move on, but instead of complying, the prisoner leapt from the shadows and attacked the armed American. The German swung at the guard and hit his hand with the club, breaking the guard's knuckles. Backing up in pain the guard again ordered his attacker, described as a "young boy of probably less than 25," to halt. When the German again lunged at the guard, the American officer fired his weapon twice, wounding the German prisoner, who later recovered from his wounds. The POWs attacked at least two other guards during the melee, one with a rock and another with a club.[17]

While the fighting went on in the street, one of the primary targets of the night's attack, an anti-Nazi Catholic priest, received a brutal beating inside his barracks. According to the reports, the priest had a pillowcase placed over his head and "suffered unmentionable brutalism and tortures at the hands of the Nazis."[18] The Nazis commonly used a pillow case to cover their victim's heads, which prevented the identification of the attackers. This tactic became so common, in fact, that it entered the prisoner lexicon as a visit from *die heilige Geist* or the "Holy Ghost." Interestingly, following the victim's transfer to an anti-Nazi camp, a hardline Nazi priest replaced him, identified in reports from 1945 as a ringleader in troublemaking, and an incorrigible Nazi.[19]

The fallout from the riot was swift. The camp's leadership quickly transferred the remaining anti-Nazis from Huntsville to Camp McCain, while those in the hospital followed, after recovering from their injuries. Camp officials also transferred at least 80 other prisoners deemed troublemakers to Camp Mexia immediately following the riot, as a temporary means of segregation. The wounded German who attacked the American guard was imprisoned pending court martial along with two others who had struck US officers. All three attackers, identified as Werner Boesch, Herbert Hoeber, and Walter Schimikowski, stood before courts-martial on February 7, 1944. After review, on March 11, 1944, Boesch received 18 months hard labor at Fort Leavenworth and forfeiture of all pay and allowances for the period. Hoeber received a similar sentence of 12 months hard labor at Leavenworth, and forfeited his pay and allowances for the period, while Schimikowski was acquitted of all charges.[20]

Beyond courts-marshal and transfers, Camp Huntsville also changed command. During mid-December 1943, Colonel John W. Crissy replaced Colonel Carvolth as the commanding officer. Crissy, who remained in command of Camp Huntsville until 1945, also brought with him a new Executive Officer, Lieutenant Colonel Alfred Oliver, who replaced Lieutenant Colonel Fredrick Baird.[21] Crissy's brand of leadership quickly came in for praise by the Swiss Legation's representative Dr. Rudolph Fischer and the U.S. Department of State official Eldon F. Nelson, who conducted inspections of the camp. Following their visit in April 1944, Nelson wrote in his report that "the situation in general in this camp has improved greatly since the last visit and that the new camp commander and his staff are interested in the welfare of the prisoners of war as well as in the good administration of the camp."[22]

Despite the improvements however, trouble continued. As noted in the same report, prisoners refused to work, and labor details were observed, "proceeding at a snail's pace." Work slowdowns and stoppages would remain a continual problem for the remainder of the camp's life, but compared to the riotous violence of November 1943, both at Camp Huntsville and around the nation, the occasional work stoppage was a minor issue.[23]

Dedication

The study of history is more than just a recording of past events. The true historian tries to understand the c a u s e s of past events and the e f f e c t they have had on our civilization today. You, Mr. Thill, are such a historian.

A good instructor seeks to impart knowledge to his students and, in addition, to inspire the student to continue to learn on his own. You, Mr. Thill, are such an instructor.

We, the students of Grand View College, do dedicate the 1965 Viking to you, Mr. Rudolf Thill, an able historian and an effective instructor.

Twenty years after his captivity at Camp Huntsville, Rudolf Thill's students at Grand View College in Des Moines, Iowa dedicated the 1965 yearbook to him. Courtesy, Grand View College, Viking, 1965.

Nazi Control Continues After the Riot

Despite improvements at Camp Huntsville, the administration remained complicit in creating some of its own problems. As noted in a previous chapter, the established practice at most POW camps in the United States was to allow the prisoners to select their own representatives to interact with the American administration, and these decisions tended to follow existing rank structure and fall under Nazi control. It was also standard procedure, as guard Titus Fields remembered, for guards to turn troublesome inmates over to the German leadership for discipline, with punishment and discipline left up to the prisoners themselves. The fact that such practices were a direct contravention of U.S. regulations did not deter such actions prior the riot.[24]

Even after the events of November 1943, local practices in Huntsville continued to mirror larger problems around the nation. So much so that on March 24, 1944, the Adjutant General of the Army issued a memorandum to all Service Commands addressing the issue and ordering the removal of spokesmen and supervisors found to be "exercising unauthorized control" and forbidding U.S. commanders from delegating any command or disciplinary functions, including command of any prisoner formations, to other individuals. Compliance varied, but it turned out that the Germans had other means of control.[25]

Within the camp itself, protected personnel, such as medical and religious members of the German military, held unique positions. By mid 1945, these were the only German officers at Camp Huntsville, and they were well-known Nazis. Their distinctive position within the camp allowed them to interact with all the prisoners at each compound, thus empowering them to exert effective control over the camp. When combined with the means to control communication, like the Nazi-controlled postal system at nearby Camp Hearne, the Nazis had definite advantages that allowed them to communicate, coordinate, and administer control outside of the view of their captors, who often turned a blind eye anyway.

In fact, Nazi leaders at Camp Huntsville often disguised their subtle forms of resistance as acts that enforced German discipline and order. For instance, they often conducted drill practice, marching in formation on camp parade fields. This outward display of order and discipline disguised both Nazi control and resistance to occupation. The "beautiful singing" of marching Germans, which was indecipherable to non-German speaking guards, often included Nazi

Canteen coupons for the PX at Camp Huntsville. Courtesy, Walker County Historical Commission.

political songs. Drill and ceremony practice, in addition to classes on "professional military" subjects conducted by the prisoners, served to remind prisoners that they were members of the German armed forces. Thus, the Nazis maintained the appearance of outward order to please the administration, but the camp administration's acquiescence to such activity had consequences. The Nazis achieved control over dissenters, anti-Nazis, criminals, and collaborators through intimidation and violence.[26]

As the war dragged on, and less disciplined troops from the battlefields of Italy and France entered camps under the control of the Nazis, problems became more acute. By the time of the D-Day landing in Normandy in June 1944, the Eastern Front had consumed much of the *Wehrmacht*. Troops captured in Europe were likely to be more realistic about Germany's future, whereas those captured during the period of German success, like the members of the *Afrika Korps*, distrusted what they viewed as defeatism. By early 1945, Nazi violence, threats, and intimidation fell on many elements, not just a few radical elements from a penal battalion. Yet, despite their dwindling numbers

A soldier sitting alone in one of the dining halls at Camp Huntsville. Courtesy, *Houston Chronicle*.

as a percentage of the prisoner population, the Nazis never lost control over the POW camp system.

Despite the violence and intimidation wrought by Nazis, murders were rare in the POW system. Officially, there were four murders and three homicides at six camps during the war, only six of which resulted in courts-martial, none at Camp Huntsville. However, Huntsville did see its share of suicide, including one after the riot. Nationwide, 22 of the 72 total suicides occurred under suspicious circumstances, but with no hard evidence to support criminal charges implicating Nazi intimidation. Yet many prisoner accounts include stories of horrific murders carried out by Nazis. Like urban myths, these may had originated in real events, but in captivity, such stories took on a life of their own. As the stories spread, they served to reinforce Nazi control.[27]

Nazi resistance at Camp Huntsville took less extreme forms as well. While drill and the singing of Nazi political songs was part of a larger program of continued indoctrination, it was largely undetected as a means of resistance. Not all forms of defiance were so subtle. Inspectors of the camp reported regular display of national emblems like the Swastika on the walls of barracks as well as portraits of Nazi leaders. Work slowdowns, stoppages, and outright strikes amongst enlisted men and volunteer non-commissioned officers were also common at the camp.[28]

In fact, Nazi elements also prevented many prisoners from attending religious services at Camp Huntsville. Such actions were more than apolitical expression of Nazi ideology. They demonstrated Nazi control and also prevented POWs from finding a peaceful outlet for the frustrations of captivity and worries about those back home. By convincing prisoners to eschew religious expression, the Nazis had a source of anger and frustration to channel toward their own ends. A prisoner comforted by the grace of God and a sure place in heaven was less likely to fear the temporal threat of Nazi intimidation. And, later in the war, when religious attendance appears to have increased at Camp Huntsville according to existing reports, those same reports note the Nazi sympathies of German chaplains.[29]

Colonel Joseph R. Carvolth assumed command of Camp Huntsville in April 1943. Born and educated in Pennsylvania, he was a veteran of World War I, and had served in General Douglas MacArthur's Rainbow Division. Carvolth was in command at Camp Huntsville during the Riot of November 1943, but was moved from the site the following month. He was transferred to Camp Mexia and then to Camp Hereford. At Hereford, critics of Carvolth accused him of allowing the prisoners to starve. For more on those accusations see, Donald Mace Williams, *Italian POWs and a Texas Church. The Murals of St. Mary's* (Lubbock, Texas: Texas Tech University Press, 1992), 75-76. Courtesy, Jeffrey L. Littlejohn.

CHAPTER IV. THE ETHICS OF GERMAN RE-EDUCATION

With Bradley Trefz, Carolyn Carroll, and Sharla Morning

The Roots of the German Re-Education Campaign

By 1944, the U.S. Army recognized that Nazi violence at the nation's prisoner of war (POW) camps posed a serious threat to the entire system. Estimates suggested that roughly forty percent of German POWs in the United States were pro-Nazi, with ten percent labeled "fanatic," and thirty percent marked as "deeply sympathetic" to the Nazi effort. At Camp Huntsville, local leaders suggested that the number of confirmed Nazis may have been even higher.[1] In fact, the continuing Nazi problem around the United States motivated the Adjutant General of the Army to issue an order on February 6, 1944, calling for the segregation of the most dangerous pro-Nazi non-commissioned officers (NCOs), especially those who had refused to cooperate with American commanders or intimidated other prisoners. This order had a particularly significant impact at Camp Huntsville, since it housed many troublesome NCOs who were "indoctrinated completely with the Nazi theory of discipline."[2]

The American effort to control Nazi elements also led to a comprehensive revision of the policies and procedures for dealing with POWs in 1944. The War Department alone issued fifty-four separate policy memoranda on POWs as well as a new version of the Military Policy manual with a greatly expanded section on POW operations and handling. Beyond doctrinal changes, the Provost Marshal General's Office (PMGO) and the Army Service Forces (ASF) deluged the POW camps with a flurry of directives throughout 1944. Taken together, these various documents created a year of change and uncertainty for camp administrators. The process became so complicated, in fact, that by the end of the year Technical Manual 19-500, "Enemy Prisoners of War," was created to present and formalize all of the various pronouncements, changes, and addenda.[3]

Among the most important innovations that emerged as part of the 1944 reorganization effort was the program to re-educate German POWs. This project had its origins in March 1943, when the U.S. Army Chief of Staff, General George C. Marshall, asked Brigadier General Frederick Osborn, Chief of the Morale Branch of the War Department, to create a program that would counter Nazi influence in the prisoner of war camps. Osborn then directed the drafting of a re-education program, which was submitted to the U.S. Provost Marshal General's Office for approval. This draft encountered criticism as soon as it was finished, however. In June 1943, as new POWs camps entered the construction process and soldiers began the training regimen, PMGO Allen Guillon dismissed the re-education idea as a waste of time and resources. Many scholars have speculated that the intense rivalry between the War Department and the Provost Marshal's office was the real reason that the re-education proposal was not initially approved.[4]

Guillon was not the only opponent of the re-education idea, however. Senior officials within the Air Force strongly opposed the program out of fear that it violated international law.[5] Articles 4 and 43 of the 1929 Geneva Convention governed the treatment of POWs and stated that all attempts to politically indoctrinate prisoners were forbidden. This prohibition, as well as the treatment of American POWs in German camps, ranked as high concerns to the Air Force, which was quick to voice its opposition to anything that might cause German retaliation. Making liberal or social democrats out of Nazis, however noble, might be viewed as a form of indoctrination and violate the letter of the international accords signed by both the United States and Germany.[6]

Pressure Mounts for Re-Education

While the U.S. military discussed the merits of re-education behind closed doors, events in the nation's POW camps sparked a national controversy over Nazi violence and the need for prisoner re-education. Between October 1943 and February 1944, national news organizations covered what appeared to be a coordinated campaign of Nazi threats, beatings, and murders of anti-Nazi prisoners. The November 1943 riot at Camp Huntsville featured in this coverage, as did a provocative statement by local Army chaplain Maurice M. Hall. Speaking before the Baptist General Convention in Dallas, Texas, Hall called the Nazis at Camp Huntsville a "treacherous, mad, and fanatical" group of men who often tried "at night in their barracks to lynch their comrades who are not Nazis." Indeed, Hall told the assembled crowd of ministers in Dallas that, "[u]nless we evangelize these men they will return to Germany after the war with nothing but contempt for our ideals, more than eager to fight another war."[7]

Hall's speech found its way into dozens of newspapers across the country and was read by thousands of people, including the celebrated journalist and war correspondent, William L. Shirer. In a January 1944 article in the *Washington Post*, Shirer quoted at length from Hall's statement as he issued his own call for the re-education of German POWs. "I may be wrong," Shirer wrote, "but in as much as the President says we are going to stamp out Nazism in Germany and the Vice President says we are going to re-educate the master-race, I've been wondering whether it wouldn't be possible and perhaps even desirable to begin right here at home with the specimens we have in the German prisoner of war camps." From Shirer's perspective, there was "nothing in the Geneva Convention" prohibiting such a re-education program, and it might even reduce violence and usher in a "return to sanity" in the camps.[8]

Despite Shirer's early advocacy for a re-education program, it was journalist Dorothy Thompson who emerged as the effort's most important spokesperson. Like Shirer, Thompson had formerly worked as a foreign correspondent in Germany documenting the rise of the Nazis for American readers. She was expelled by Hitler in 1934, however, and returned to the United States to continue her anti-Nazi campaign in a syndicated column called "On the Record." In an April 26, 1944 article, Thompson complained that the U.S. government had not moved fast enough to solve the Nazi problem that had emerged in POW camps over the previous year. She noted that stories of Nazis murdering anti-Nazis had been corroborated, and that camp administrators had allowed Nazis to celebrate Hitler's birthday and even use the Nazi salute. Thompson found these stories outrageous and argued that the American government was "going farther than the obligations of the Geneva Convention" required. Indeed, she said, "How do we like the boast that American prison camps are training centers for the coming Nazi underground?"[9]

Later in spring 1944, Thompson joined a committee of like-minded journalists, professors, and religious leaders who supported the creation of a re-education program for German POWs. Led by Gerhart Seger, the editor of a German-American newspaper, *Neue Volkszeitung*, the committee included Dr. Monroe Deutsch, vice-president of the University of California, Louis Lochner, former chief of the Associated Press in Berlin, and Dr. George H. Schuster, president of Hunter College. This prestigious cross-section of American citizens pressured the U.S. government to carry out a more comprehensive segregation program that would separate Nazi and anti-Nazi prisoners in POW camps and begin to re-educate the most compliant prisoners based on the "ideals of democracy."[10]

Meanwhile, Thompson launched an even more important behind-the-scenes effort on her own. As a good friend of First Lady Eleanor Roosevelt, Thompson shared her concerns about Nazi violence and the need for POW re-education with the White House. Alarmed by what Thompson told her, Mrs. Roosevelt promptly scheduled two dinner conversations with Major Maxwell McKnight, the Administrative Head of POW Operations, to confirm that Thompson's stories were true. After McKnight assured the First Lady that the reports of Nazi violence were accurate, Mrs. Roosevelt responded indignantly: "I've got to talk to Franklin. Right in our backyard, to have these Nazis moved in and controlling the whole thought process!" She thought that it was disgraceful.[11]

Mrs. Roosevelt wasted no time in meeting with her husband, and he quickly agreed that the POW issue needed to be addressed. In short order, the President called upon the Secretaries of War and State, Henry Stimson and Edward Stettinius Jr., to solve the problem, and they in turn contacted the newly appointed Provost Marshal General, Archer L. Lerch. The PMGO then revived Brigadier General Osborn's plan for a re-education program that had been shelved a year earlier. This plan stipulated that Nazi and anti-Nazi POWs should be separated within American camps and that re-education of the most amenable prisoners should begin right away. An important stipulation was added to the program at this time, stating that all participation must be voluntary in order to avoid possible violation of the Geneva Convention. Secretary of War Stimson insisted that "it was essential to the success of such a program that it shall be carried through without publicity." The public thus knew nothing about the re-education program that began officially on April 8, 1944, and the U.S. military took steps to keep it that way until after the war.[12]

The German Re-education Program Gets Underway

In order to justify the new re-education program for German POWs, the War Department began looking for legal proof that it was humane and necessary. A loophole in Article 17 of the Geneva

Convention, which stated that belligerent powers should "encourage intellectual diversions" for prisoners of war, provided sufficient cover.[13] In fact, the military officially titled the new re-education effort a special project for intellectual diversion and developed a curriculum that emphasized pro-American and pro-democratic materials. Geneva Convention protocols notwithstanding, proponents of re-education believed that the threat posed by massive numbers of enemy captives on American soil warranted the risks. They also felt that prisoners should gain at least a cursory understanding of American society and politics to counteract totalitarianism. Further support for the program came from surveys conducted by the Intelligence Section of the Psychological Warfare Division, which showed that German soldiers continued to have confidence in Hitler's leadership abilities even as the war turned in favor of the Allies. Several surveys conducted in

Major John W. Crissy (second from left) initially served in Huntsville as the Commanding Officer of the Army Administration School at Sam Houston State Teachers College. In December 1943, he returned to town to assume command of Camp Huntsville following the riot that occurred that November. Crissy remained in command of the camp through August 1945. Courtesy, University of Oregon, *Oregana*, 1969.

Major Maxwell S. McKnight speaking at Fort Benning, Georgia. Courtesy, U.S. Army.

A teacher lecturing in the German re-education program. Courtesy, U.S. Army.

prisoner of war camps showed that German soldiers shared a fierce loyalty to Hitler and Nazi beliefs, even months after being held.[14]

With justification tentatively established for the re-education program, the Provost Marshal General's office created the Prisoner of War Special Projects Division to oversee the effort. Lieutenant Colonel Edward Davison, a nationally known poet, teacher, and author, led the project, and he soon convened a small group of American professors and anti-Nazi German intellectuals to create the guidelines for the program. The group first established a mission and goals, which stated that the "prisoners would be given facts, objectively presented but so selected and assembled as to correct misinformation and prejudices surviving Nazi conditioning." In particular, the facts were to be "made available through such media as literature, motion pictures, newspapers, music, art and educational courses" that would demonstrate both "the impracticality and viciousness of the Nazi position" as well as the soundness of the American "democratic system of government."[15]

Given these goals, the architects of the program incorporated pieces of American culture—literature, music, art, movies, and politics—into a comprehensive collection, which was to be made available within the camps for voluntary use. Ultimately, the program exposed participating German soldiers to democratic ideals and to the knowledge that many countries, not just America, practiced some form of democracy. The early leaders of the re-education effort initially worked from a New York base, but later moved to a permanent location in Rhode Island, where the organization became known as the "Idea Factory" or just the "Factory." The directors of the "Factory" offered training sessions to officers from the POW camps in the summer of 1944 to familiarize them with both the Intellectual Diversion Program and the German language. They knew that the success of their effort depended upon having a qualified staff at the camps to oversee the re-education effort and to monitor the reactions of the soldiers.[16]

The most visible result of the German re-education program was a national newspaper, *Der Ruf* (*The Call*), written by German POWs and circulated throughout the camp system. The paper appeared bimonthly with high-quality illustrations and was intended to give "the German Prisoner . . . realistic news of all important military and political events, a true picture of the German homefront, . . . entertainment and a true understanding of the American way of life."[17] The leaders of the "Factory" closely monitored the reactions of German soldiers at the camps to see if the paper would win a following, while the military closely inspected POW mail for any mention of the newspaper for the first five issues. Although some soldiers saw the newspaper as nothing more than "Jewish propaganda," others expressed great interest in the information presented and read it regularly.[18]

The Re-education Program in Action at Camp Huntsville

The re-education effort at Camp Huntsville proceeded slowly. To begin with, the prisoners took part in the production of their own "lively" publication, *Die Fanfare*, which the men greatly enjoyed. The editions of this paper contained news excerpts, pieces of educational interest, book reviews, and sports stories. The men even wrote articles on job safety and method instruction for prisoner labor, which, in turn, helped the war effort. Although this publication was briefly suspended due to the military's prohibition on the use of mimeograph machines, it was eventually re-opened and found to be a positive form of expression for the prisoners.[19]

In addition to this local paper, POWs also enjoyed the opportunity to take classes from their fellow prisoners at Camp Huntsville. Since late 1943, POWs had offered and participated in courses on English, history, government, and business, among other topics. The leaders of the Intellectual Diversion Program intended to harness these activities to teach the prisoners about American values and democratic traditions. To do so, the leaders of the "Factory" wanted American administrators and college educators to take over the teaching responsibilities in the POW courses.

At Camp Huntsville, this transition took time. When the Special Projects Division sent Captain Alexander Lakes to report on developments at the camp in February 1945, he found that the local Assistant Executive Officer, Captain Alton Brady, had not yet hired a director of studies, paid instructors, or informed the prisoners that they could take correspondence courses. Lakes suggested that Brady immediately address each of these issues, and soon thereafter Lt. Colonel Davison, the director of the Special Projects Division, contacted President Harmon Lowman at Huntsville's Sam Houston State Teachers College (SHSTC) to request his help in the matter. In a March 1945 letter, Davison asked Lowman to assist camp personnel with the selection of books and the design of educational programming by creating a college committee to work with camp officials. A few weeks later, Lowman appointed Dr. L. A. McGee, professor of government, as chairman of the new committee, which soon set to work organizing general education classes at the camp

"The Growth of Democracy," from the booklet, *Wille und Weg*. This is a typical example of the material used in the German re-education program. Courtesy, U.S. Army.

to provide for democratic training. In fact, the prisoners soon got a chance to put these ideas into practice, when camp administrators hosted an election for prisoner representatives by secret ballot "as an experiment in democracy."[20]

As time went on, each prisoner compound at Camp Huntsville developed an extensive library that contained books on the "American Spirit." These texts, which Hitler had banned in Germany, were placed on the shelves for POWs, while books by German authors that were considered "undemocratic" were removed.[21] Some of the POWs favorite books, which were distributed by "the Factory," included *Amerika* by Stephen Vincent Benet, *Achtung Europa* (*Attention Europe*), *Lotte in Weimer* (*The Beloved Returns*) and *Wem die Stunde schlägt* (*For Whom the Bell Toll*) by Ernest Hemingway. The other books and periodicals most sought after in Camp Huntsville included business and medical surveys, as well as the *New York Times* and *Houston Chronicle*. In addition to these items, the "Factory" wrote and published its own text for German soldiers: *Kleiner Führer durch Amerika* (*A Brief Guide Through America*). This book was an instant success with German soldiers as a souvenir of America. It was a standard item found in their luggage when repatriation allowed them to return to Germany. The Special Projects Division felt that the books provided to the POWs might help affect postwar Germany in the long term in that many of the books would return to Germany in the hands of former prisoners who wanted to see a change for the better.[22]

Realizing that books were not the only medium of entertainment or education used by the soldiers, the PMGO also appreciated the power of film to persuade prisoners. Concerned that many popular films being shown in American theaters presented the country as an immoral and lawless place, the Special Projects Division removed films such as *Lady Scarface*, *Millionaire Playboy*, *Legion of the Lawless*, *Wolf Man*, and *Too Many Blondes* from circulation.[23] In their place, administrators set up an elaborate film program that portrayed America as a compelling example of democracy. The most important films in the new re-

A view of the theater at Holloran General Hospital, as German prisoners of war watched the screening of official U.S. Army films showing the victims of Nazi atrocities who died by the thousands from starvation and disease in the various concentration camps. Many prisoners covered their eyes as they watched the horrible scenes, while others still smiled in arrogant indifference. Courtesy Associated Press.

education program were the *Why We Fight* series by Hollywood director Frank Capra and other films taken by the U.S. military depicting the war's atrocities such as the Holocaust. The POWs had mixed feelings about these films, but apparently enjoyed pieces that emphasized life in America and the role that freedom and democracy played in the average citizen's life.[24]

Successes and Failures of the Re-education Program

From one perspective, the re-education program enjoyed several important successes. According to reports, the combination of Germany's surrender and the first six months of the Intellectual Diversion program resulted in a new spirit among German POWs. They denounced Hitler and their former allegiance to National Socialism, while signing petitions pledging their support to help form a new democratic Germany upon their return home. Some POWs even created charity funds to support the displaced children of Europe, while others offered to help the American Army defeat Japan in the Pacific.[25] Scholar Judith Gansberg referred to the Special Project Division's Intellectual Diversion Program as "one of the most remarkable and successful training programs ever implemented under the auspices of the military."[26] Indeed, the United States was a pioneer in re-education because no other countries had attempted such a program during World War II. From another perspective, however, the re-education program represented an arrogant and futile attempt by America to convert Nazis to a new worldview.[27] Scholars who share this position emphasize that the program probably had only a minimal influence on those soldiers who were never fully indoctrinated into the ideology of National Socialism and who did not see Hitler as a hero. For other prisoners, the true Nazis, the program was meaningless.[28]

Re-education also ironically underscored the shortcomings of American democracy, especially in the South. As white soldiers and educators at Camp Huntsville taught Nazi prisoners about the finer points of democracy, African Americans in the state lived under a discriminatory regime of white supremacy that degraded and disenfranchised them. In fact, stories from the period demonstrate that East Texas was one of the most prejudiced and dangerous areas in the nation for African Americans. For instance, white law enforcement officers in the area often faced accusations that they engaged in police brutality against African American citizens in an effort to demonstrate their authority. In one 1938 case, for example, a white highway patrolman "insulted, humiliated, and slapped" Dr. G.L. Prince, the black President of the National Baptist Convention, on Highway 75 north of Huntsville because the minister apparently refused to exhibit the proper subservience. Later, another infamous example came in the case of convicted murderer Nehemiah Glover, an African American prisoner in Huntsville, who sought and was granted a brief reprieve from execution by Supreme Court Justice Felix Frankfurter because he alleged that he had been "beaten, kicked and 'whipped' with a rubber hose by police officers" to get a confession. Ultimately, Glover was executed on January 28, 1942, but the accusations of police brutality did not end there. In another story from the period, Robert Harris, a black citizen of New Waverly, accused the sheriff of Huntsville, Ben Small, of beating him on July 22, 1944, the date of the Democratic primary election. According to Harris and an initial report in the *Houston Informer*, Small's action resulted from a "disturbance of the peace" call, which had been prompted by Harris's attempt to cast his ballot in the primary (only months after the Supreme Court's landmark ruling outlawing the white primary in *Smith v. Allwright*). When Small arrived at the scene, Harris said the officer beat him and took him to the county jail. Small denied the story and successfully sued the *Houston Informer* for publishing its account of the event, but white election officials and law enforcement officers continued to keep African Americans out of the political system.[29]

In fact, Camp Huntsville sat in the middle of one of the nation's least democratic congressional districts during World War II. The Seventh Texas Congressional District had a total population of 299,721, but only 11,139 of those residents (or 3.7 percent) voted during 1942. In similar fashion, out of a statewide population of 6,414,824 in 1940, only 274,627 (or 4.28 percent) voted in the national election. These dismal voting percentages resulted from the widespread use of the poll tax, which charged people to vote far in advance of the actual election. There was a national movement afoot during the period to abolish the poll tax, or to at least allow servicemen fighting overseas to bypass it when casting their votes, but Congressman Nat Patton from the Seventh Texas felt compelled to vote against even this modest effort to eliminate the poll tax for soldiers because of the local racial situation. It seems that any crack in the political structure of Jim Crow was too dangerous a move, even for those teaching democracy to their sworn enemies.[30]

Ironically, some of the soldiers assigned to the POW camps were black, and many of them "frequently contrasted the treatment of German POWs with their own treatment and reported in countless letters that 'there are German prisoners here and they live better than we do.'[31] Although we have uncovered no record of any black soldiers serving as guards at Camp Huntsville, many local African Americans recall the discriminatory treatment that they received during the period and compare it with the dignified and humane treatment offered the German POWs. For instance, Richard Watkins, a resident of Huntsville, says that "the reason" his father—a Lieutenant Colonel in World War II—left Walker County and refused to return was because of local racism. "[T]o see the German prisoners treated better than he was," Watkins says, "was just something he couldn't get over."[32]

Most infuriating, though, was the knowledge, eventually confirmed, that the American prisoners of war held in Axis countries were not being accorded the same care and rights as their German counterparts in Huntsville and other camps. The attention to the Geneva Convention could not have been less reciprocal, and these disparities came very close to home when native sons of Huntsville itself were captured behind enemy lines. For instance, the Baccus family of Huntsville initially received an anodyne and obviously censored letter via the Red Cross from their son, Sargent Robert E. Baccus, who had been shot down over northern Italy and captured by the Nazis in 1944. Nonetheless, the ugly details of Sgt. Baccus's

German POWs preparing a Camp Newspaper, *Die PW Woche*, like the Camp Huntsville paper, *Die Fanfare*. Courtesy, U.S. Army.

captivity did emerge after his liberation. His troubles apparently began from the get-go: while just fifteen miles from Allied lines, Sgt. Baccus was betrayed by a local priest sympathetic to the Germans and was then taken to Stalag Luft 1 near Barth, Germany. Far from enjoying the conditions of the later television fantasy "Hogan's Heroes" set in a POW camp, Sgt. Baccus was kept in solitary confinement for the first week and was also grilled over the treatment of Germans in the Huntsville camp. He told his captors the truth—that he knew nothing about camp conditions. After that harsh beginning, things only got worse with deepening food and water shortages caused by the unraveling of the Third Reich in the first few months of 1945. Between February 15 and March 27, 1945, no Red Cross supplies arrived at Stalag Luft 1, and the men were forced to eat feral cats, turnips, potato scraps, and rotten horse meat to survive that difficult stretch. Even when the Red Cross supplies resumed in late March and April 1945, the meager and monotonous diet of tiny portions of Spam, milk, cheese, sardines, vitamin pills, and graham crackers with peanut butter was barely enough for subsistence. In addition, the Germans gave the prisoners very little to do as well as very little to eat. Baccus and his

German POWs at Camp Huntsville made this doll bed for Charles F. Parker of Trinity. Parker worked at the camp as an electrician and had a young daughter, Kathleen. The cut out figures on the bed are German fairy tale characters. Courtesy Kathleen Newman Skains.

comrades had to develop their own classes and amusements; this was in sharp contrast to America's attempted re-education schedules.[33]

While Baccus and his comrades fended for themselves during Germany's collapse, Huntsville natives captured by the Japanese had equally harrowing (or worse) tales of treatment to tell. For example, Major Eula Fails, a U.S. Army nurse and Sam Houston State College graduate, was captured during the fall of the Philippines in 1942. She went on to contract beriberi and tuberculosis while imprisoned for almost three years at Santo Thomas, a university campus; her health would never completely recover. Major Fails, though, was relatively lucky in that she did not have to endure or to witness the horrors of the Bataan death march, a grueling torture that killed many American and Filipino captives. There were obvious reasons, then, why no one in the Axis countries envied the Allied prisoners' fate, in sharp contrast to the carping about the feeding and "feting" of German prisoners in the Huntsville and other American camps.[34]

Final Assessments of Camp Huntsville's German POW Program

When the last Germans left Camp Huntsville in 1945, the camp administration had largely managed to weather the storm. While the Nazis still exerted some measure of control, reports demonstrated that the camp administration was firmly on top of the situation, regularly identifying the ringleaders and implementing solutions.[35] In the final assessment, Camp Huntsville, like many camps during the war, found a way to muddle through, despite bureaucratic problems, personnel issues, and structural failings. Like the rest of the war effort, the men and women who worked at Camp Huntsville accomplished their tasks, with a steep learning curve that produced its share of pain for those involved.

Given the scale of the operation, however, it may be argued that the administrators and soldiers at Camp Huntsville achieved something amazing in just a few years' time. They successfully confined thousands of enemy combatants in the midst of the United States with only one major incident over a 3-year period. It is sometimes easy to forget, amidst tales of friendly Germans quietly hoeing cotton, that some of those enemy combatants were hardened, fanatical enemies of the United States and its way of life. Yet during the life of Camp Huntsville, none successfully escaped, and any violence or action by the prisoners remained confined to internal power struggles within the camp.

CHAPTER V. JAPANESE PRISONERS, RE-EDUCATION, AND THE CLOSING OF CAMP HUNTSVILLE

With Natalie Miles and Patricia Hale

Changing Focus

Nelda Woodall felt a sense of elation when she heard the news in May 1945 that World War II in Europe was finally over. American and allied forces had defeated the last remnants of the Nazi Army in Germany, and her son, Master Sergeant William Ross Woodall, had been awarded the Bronze Star for "meritorious action" in combat. Yet, Woodall was no Pollyanna. As editor of the local *Huntsville Item*, she knew that any hope for a swift and decisive end to the war in the Pacific was unlikely to be realized. Put simply, wresting victory from the Japanese empire would require both discipline and sacrifice. "We haven't yet locked with the main force of the enemy," she told her readers on May 24, two weeks after V-E Day. "As we get closer to the heart of the Jap empire, our task is becoming harder and tougher."[1]

As Woodall encouraged her neighboring Huntsvillians to continue their support for the Pacific War effort, developments abroad promised to reshape the local landscape and introduce a new Japanese presence to the Huntsville community. These changes had their origins in the work of John K. Emmerson, a State Department officer and East Asian specialist, who formulated a plan in early 1945 to re-educate Japanese prisoners of war (POWs) and use them in "front-line propaganda activities" to help end World War II. As an American emissary in the China-Burma-India theater, Emmerson knew that the United States had turned over the vast majority of its Japanese POWs to the Commonwealth of Australia. He knew also, however, that roughly 5,000 Japanese POWs with "potential military intelligence value" were living in the continental United States in 1945. Based on his first-hand experience with a re-education program he had witnessed among communist revolutionaries in Yan'an, China in 1944,

Emmerson officially proposed his own project in April 1945. The Provost Marshal General subsequently approved the concept, which military leaders considered an extension of the ongoing Intellectual Diversion Program then being used to re-educate German prisoners in POW camps around the nation. In September 1945, following the atomic bombing and official surrender of Japan, the U.S. military selected Camp Huntsville as the lone site for its re-education program for Japanese POWs. The effort, which included roughly 160 Japanese prisoners, required new leadership at Camp Huntsville and brought the faculty at nearby Sam Houston State Teachers College into a fascinating, if brief, program to shape the post-war world for the better. Although the entire project lasted only four months, the following examination of its origins, development, and outcome, suggests that it showcased both the idealism and the hubris that defined U.S. policy throughout the remainder of the American century.[2]

The Pacific Theater of War and the Origins of Japanese Re-education

In the spring of 1945, as American and allied forces concluded the final stages of the war against Hitler, U.S. military commanders turned their attention to the Pacific theater. After years of grueling and costly battles against a determined Japanese enemy, American leaders increased the size and scope of U.S. efforts in the Pacific. In March, Major General Curtis LeMay ordered 334 B-29 bombers to attack Tokyo in a devastating fire-bombing raid that destroyed 16 square miles of the city and killed more than 100,000 people. Then, a few weeks later, the U.S. Navy launched the largest amphibious assault of World War II—with more than 40 carriers, 18 battleships, and 200 destroyers—in an attempt to take control of Okinawa. Eventually, American strategists planned to use this key island location as the launching ground for B-29 raids and a full-scale invasion of Japan's home islands.[3]

Despite the terrifying power of America's military campaign in the Pacific, few people in the U.S. government believed that the war against Japan would be over in a matter of months. In fact, Japanese soldiers and civilians had regularly fought to the death or committed suicide rather than surrender to American forces. At Tarawa in the Gilbert Islands, for instance, only eight of 2,600 Japanese soldiers had survived the U.S. attack. Then, later, on Saipan in the Mariana Islands, hundreds of Japanese civilians had jumped from cliffs to kill themselves in acts of desperation to avoid capture by American forces. This tragic tactic was also embraced by more than 1,900 kamikaze pilots who sacrificed themselves in suicide attacks against the American fleet off Okinawa in May 1945, seeking to halt the U.S. effort there. Although this strategy ultimately failed, it confirmed the widely-held American belief that Japanese soldiers and civilians would stop at nothing to defend their honor and homeland. More ominously, it also demonstrated how arduous and costly an American invasion of the Japanese home islands was likely to be.[4]

As American military leaders planned the final stages of the war against Japan, a variety of U.S. diplomatic and academic experts analyzed the enemy's behavior in an attempt to coordinate both the end of the war and the planning of the post-war era. Following the lead of influential thinkers, like Franz Boas, Margaret Mead, and Ruth Benedict, anthropologists of the period encouraged policy makers to reject commonly held American stereotypes that portrayed the Japanese as mindless drones following their god-emperor, and to instead view them as devoted warriors who were products of their own educational, political, and cultural surroundings. This new interpretation of the Japanese, historian John Dower has written, provided that their national character was not racially fixed or permanent, but was, like the American character, open to change based upon new experiences and educational opportunities.[5]

A long-time disciple of this view, John Emmerson of the U.S. State Department, spent the period from October to December 1944, in the new communist capital of China, Yan'an, in support of the U.S. Army's Observation Group (or Dixie Mission), which was gathering intelligence and making connections with the revolutionary leaders of China. After meeting the top communists leaders, including Zhou Enlai, Mao Zedong, and General Chu Teh, Emmerson spent most of his time in the area with Chinese and Japanese communists who were re-educating Japanese POWs. Chief among the Japanese leaders in Yan'an was Nosaka Sanzo, a native of Yamaguchi prefecture, who had been orphaned at 14, before becoming an outspoken critic of the Japanese oligarchy and its apparent disregard for the concerns of the working people. As a young man, Sanzo attended Tokyo's Keio University and the London School of Economics, and he became a cosmopolitan Marxist theorist, who served as a founding member of both the Japanese Communist Party and the Japanese People's Emancipation League. The later organization ran a Workers and Peasants School in the caves of Yan'an to transform Japanese POWs into good communists. It was this school—with its enlightened procedures and successful indoctrination—that Emmerson hoped to emulate with Japanese POWs in the United States. Based on his first-hand experience at the school, Emmerson began to devise a plan that called for the American government to select the most compliant of the 5,000 Japanese POWs in the U.S., teach them about western-style democracy, and then persuade them to help shape the "pacification" effort and post-war "political orientation" of a democratic Japan.[6]

Few people paid Emmerson's plan any mind, until a chance meeting he had in March 1945 with Ellen Downes, an old friend from the American embassy in Tokyo, who had taken a job as the private assistant to Secretary of the Interior Harold Ickes. Within days of seeing Downes, Emmerson had a much coveted appointment with Ickes, which, in turn, resulted in meetings with John J. McCloy, the Assistant Secretary of War, and Archer L. Lerch, the Provost Marshal General. Each of these officials approved Emmerson's re-education proposal, and he quickly set out to make the project a reality.[7]

Planning the Re-education Program

At the suggestion of the Provost Marshal General, Emmerson began his effort by visiting several American POW camps in April 1945 in order to interview Japanese prisoners and familiarize himself with current operations. His stops included Camp McCoy, Wisconsin, the largest POW facility for Japanese prisoners within the U.S., and a second, smaller detention facility at Angel Island in San Francisco, California. The trip lasted from April 4 to April 30, and, during the course of his travel, Emmerson also delivered lectures on foreign policy at Northwestern University, the University of Chicago, Stanford University, and the Presidio in Monterey, California.[8]

Two figures with experience and interest in the re-education effort accompanied Emmerson on his trip. First, Major William B. Gemmill, a World War I veteran, former Chicago attorney, and member of the Executive Division of the Provost Marshal General's Office, joined the research team. Gemmill had played a significant role in the assessment of the U.S. military's German re-education program, which had begun roughly one year earlier in April 1944. In particular, Gemmill had examined German POW newspapers to assess both their usefulness as democratizing tools and their overall impact on the POW experience.[9]

Rounded up in the bitter fighting off Iwo Jima, Japan, the first Japanese prisoners of that operation are taken aboard a Coast Guard-manned invasion transport on March 9, 1945. Courtesy, Associated Press.

Dr. Charles W. Hepner, a former Lutheran missionary to Japan, served as the other member of Emmerson's group. A native of Woodstock, Virginia, Hepner held degrees from Roanoke College, Southern Theological Seminary, and Yale University. He had lived in Japan as a missionary from 1912 to 1920, had mastered the Japanese language, and had written a doctoral dissertation at Yale on "The Kurozumi Sect of Shinto." The Society for International Cultural Relations praised Hepner's scholarship on Shinto, and the Meiji Japan Society published his dissertation in 1935. Later, however, the Japanese government seized and interned Hepner and his wife, while they were serving as missionaries in Japan during the winter of 1941-1942. In fact, Hepner developed pneumonia while he was in Japanese custody, but recovered before he and his wife were released along with 219 U.S. civilians in July 1942. At that time, Hepner returned to the United States and went to work for the U.S. Office of War Information.[10]

In April 1945, Emmerson led his partners, Gemmill and

Hepner, on an assessment tour of Camp McCoy, which housed roughly 2,300 of the 5,000 Japanese POWs in the U.S. The men discovered that the site offered a well-run, if complicated, detention facility that held Japanese officers, non-commissioned officers (NCOs), and enlisted men. Although Camp McCoy's size seemed to make it the ideal place to house the Japanese re-education program, it soon became apparent that an alternate location would need to be secured. Emmerson based this belief on an April 7 conversation he had with Jiro Saito, the ranking Japanese officer in the camp, who told Emmerson that "the Japanese here did not speak much about the future and certainly . . . did not want to return to Japan after the war." Saito also expressed doubt "that any discussions of post-war problems or speculations on the political future, especially in the event of a Japanese defeat, would be profitable."[11]

On April 8, despite his misgivings, Saito brought six other officers—Shigesaburo Ando, Taiichiro Hayashi, Shuichiro Kato, Eichi Matsumoto, Makoto Otani, and Yoshio Kajishima—to meet with Emmerson and Hepner. Although all the men in the group spoke English and had a university education or its equivalent, the entire conversation was conducted in Japanese to place the POWs at ease. The officers argued that "they did not think about the possibility of Japan's defeat in this war." In fact, one said that "if Japan is defeated, it means the end of the Yamato race," while another said that "if

John K. Emmerson (center) with (l to r) Zhou Enlai, Zhu De, Mao Zedong, and Ye Jianying, Yan'an, China, 1944. Courtesy, Donald K. Emmerson.

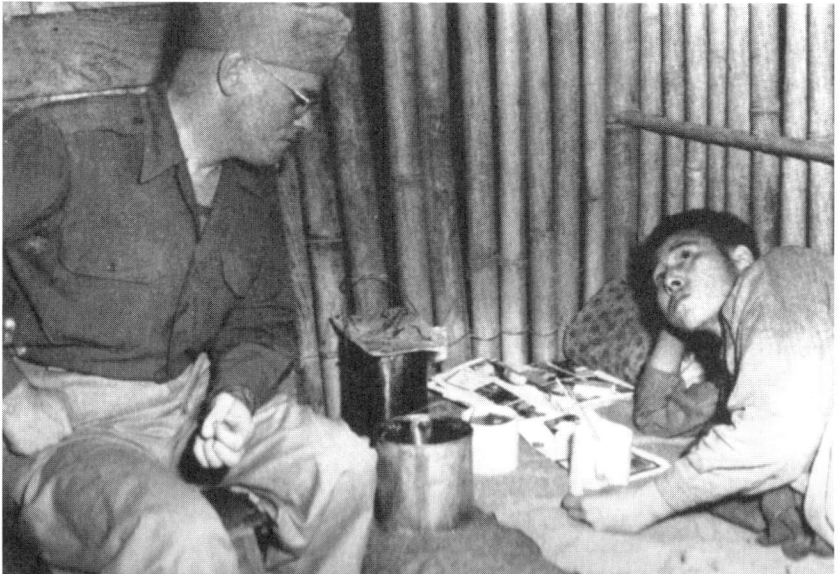

John K. Emmerson interrogating a Japanese prisoner of war in Burma, 1944.
Courtesy, Donald K. Emmerson.

the Emperor system were abolished or changed, he would commit suicide." The other officers supported the idea of "Asia for the Asiastics," and suggested that peace might be possible if a "Monroe Doctrine" for Asia was established at the end of the war. In regards to re-education, the officers expressed an interest in American institutions and democracy, which led Emmerson to suggest in his notes that an "indoctrination course" that simply provided the POWs "the opportunity to learn something about the United States might gradually lead toward a change in their fundamental attitude."[12]

On the next day, however, Emmerson found his optimism squashed. In a conversation with 13 non-commissioned officers, it became clear that the prisoners at Camp McCoy had fallen under the control of a "small clique" of Japanese NCOs led by two men named Kojima and Higashi, who "rule[d] the group with an iron hand." Apparently, Higashi dominated the conversation and argued that "all the POW's feel the same, that they have no hope for the future, and without exception, never intend to return to Japan." Higashi told Emmerson and Hepner that he and his countrymen would not begin to think about "the possibility of Japan's defeat" until "American soldiers [we]re in the streets of Tokyo." The NCOs rejected any talk of a new Japan and declared that the country's national policy or *Kokutai* would "never change." Although some of the participants in the meeting expressed interest in Japanese books on American history or institutions, they also called for reading materials on Japanese culture and history.[13]

Following their rather disheartening trip to Wisconsin, Emmerson traveled to Angel Island, California, while Hepner journeyed to Clarinda, Iowa, where a local POW camp housed several hundred Japanese prisoners.[14] In his notes on the April 12 to 14 visit at Clarinda, and a subsequent stop at the Headquarters of the Seventh Service Command in Omaha, Nebraska, Hepner suggested a possible solution to the problems that he and Emmerson had found at Camp McCoy. Specifically, he found that the segregation or division of the prisoners by rank created a more open and productive environment for political discussions. At Clarinda, where segregation was practiced, Hepner discovered that the POWs seemed to be "more responsive" and "more cooperative than those at Camp McCoy." In addition, he reported that his talks with the Commandant, members of his staff, and spokesmen for the Japanese POWs there led him to believe that "at least forty or fifty, and perhaps more [POWs], may be expected to cooperate" in the re-education program.[15]

As a result of Emmerson and Hepner's report on their investigations, the Provost Marshal General's office formally approved a "reorientation" program for Japanese POWs "along the lines of that in effect for German prisoners of war" in a memorandum dated July 5, 1945. The purpose of the program was to "impress on the minds of the Japanese prisoners of war what the attitude of a citizen of the United States is toward life and government and to create an appreciation of American principles and traditions." The program called for "the segregation of officers and noncommissioned officers from privates and the further segregation of cooperative prospects from all other groups of prisoners."[16]

Camp Huntsville and Re-educating the Japanese POWs

Although the historical record is unfortunately silent on the selection of Camp Huntsville as the home site for the Japanese re-education project, it was decided in September 1945 that all cooperative Japanese prisoners were to be sent to the Texas site, where the "reorientation" program would be housed. As the remaining

German POWs at Huntsville were transferred to other locations, it became obvious that the hiring of a new commandant, director of education, and teaching staff was necessary. Lt. Colonel Boude C. Moore, an old friend of Emmerson's, was chosen to serve as local commander at the post, where he would handle the administrative duties of the operation. Moore was particularly well-suited for this job because he was an army officer who had been born in Japan to a missionary family, spoke fluent Japanese, and did postgraduate work at the Imperial University. While Moore had lived in Japan from 1924 until 1941, he was educated in the United States and served as a lecturer at the Army's highly regarded School of Military Government at the University of Virginia in Charlottesville. In this new role, Moore would be assisted by Hepner, the far eastern specialist who had helped to plan the program and get it off the ground.[17]

Despite diligent work, Moore did have some minor problems securing staff and support at the camp. On September 29, 1945, just two weeks before the prisoners were set to arrive, the camp was struggling to find translators. Once adequate interpreters were found, it was discovered that some of the translators were simply not psychologically or linguistically qualified for the type of work that was to take place at Camp Huntsville. Once camp officials finally succeeded in finding qualified candidates, however, several of them were unable to find lodging in Huntsville, which led the military to advise the translators to report without their families. The camp officials also had to seek special permission to employ civilians such as stenographers and lecturers, and it was a challenge to get the rights to do so. While many of the issues were eventually resolved, these problems led to a rocky start for the program.[18]

As the staff was put in place, recruitment of Japanese prisoners began; however, not every Japanese prisoner was accepted into the re-education program. Those with a "desire to study American institutions and governmental forms" went through a rigorous application process, and only those who were qualified were accepted into the program.[19] When the screenings concluded, 26 officers, 36 non-commissioned officers (NCO), and 143 privates were selected to participate in the program. These 205 prisoners arrived at Camp Huntsville on October 5, 1945, and classes began right away.

Since the mentalities, ideologies, and traditions of the Japanese varied so greatly from those of the German POWs, the U.S. government realized that a new system of re-education was necessary. This system of indoctrination, as various government documents referred to it, had several objectives. First, American authorities wanted to use this project as a laboratory to test the effectiveness of propaganda in war, specifically against the Japanese enemy. The government also hoped that, by influencing the prisoners, some of them would be willing to bring democracy to Japan when the war ended. The government argued that, if the Japanese understood the American system of democracy, and saw the success that arose from it, they would be willing to help spread the democratic process around the world. It was this hope that created a system of re-education employing the best academic assets of East Texas.[20]

Working in coordination with Boude Moore and Charles Hepner were a Japanese-speaking chaplain, William A. McIlwaine, as well as First Lieutenants, Bennie H. Scarpero and John F. O'Brien. In addition to these personnel, the government also drew upon the resources and professors at nearby Sam Houston State Teacher's College (SHSTC).[21] In all, there were five professors from various disciplines at SHSTC who contributed their time and knowledge to the re-education program. Dr. Joseph Clark, a professor of history and director of the social sciences, lectured on topics such as the development of representative government and how democracy

Charles W. Hepner (third from left) led the Japanese re-education program at Camp Huntsville. Courtesy, Muhlenberg College, *Ciarla*, 1951.

Camp McCoy, Wisconsin. Courtesy, Linda M. Fournier, Fort McCoy Public Affairs.

came to America. Dr. F.A. McCray, a professor and the director of vocational agriculture, discussed items such as the agricultural programs in the United States. Dr. L.A. McGee, a professor of government, delivered lectures on the origins of the American economic system as well as how the system functioned. Dr. M.B. Measemer, an associate professor of geography, gave a number of lectures that traced the expansion of American democracy and the relationships between social democracy and nationalism. Dr. Donald W. Mitchell, a professor of government, gave six lectures to the prisoners on the following topics: liberty and human rights; past and present democracies; and branches of American government and the accompanying separation of powers.[22]

These professors from SHSTC and other guest speakers such as Chaplain McIlwaine and Dr. Hepner allotted two and a half hours for their lectures, and structured the classes so that they followed an outline summary. Each paragraph or point of their lecture was first presented in English, and then was translated into Japanese for the prisoners. Once a lecture was completed, the students had the opportunity to have a discussion with the professor and ask any questions about the material. On some occasions, these discussions led to group work in which the students went deeper into the subjects. These conversations covered a variety of topics that ranged from the beginnings of democracy in classical antiquity to its practical applications in the mid-twentieth century. More theoretical lectures, such as the necessity of a free mind in the search for truth and the main points in the Declaration of Independence, were put forth in

Japanese prisoners at Camp McCoy, Wisconsin. Courtesy, Linda M. Fournier, Fort McCoy Public Affairs.

an attempt to highlight particular flaws in the Japanese ideology and to emphasize distinguishing characteristics of democracy.[23]

The program, while initially successful, was not without problems. To begin with, many of the Japanese POWs did not like the materials being presented and distrusted the American leaders of the program. Camp officials had hoped that they could have avoided this situation, since they had truthfully stated to the prisoners the purpose of the program; however, many of the prisoners still felt that they were being deceived. The Japanese were also defensive when lecturers referred to Japanese morals and institutions. Many of the prisoners found solace in both Japanese ideology and the imperial system and were afraid of losing face with the other POWs in the camp. It was also difficult for these prisoners to see the system that they had fought for to be deemed inferior in comparison to the United States.[24]

To counteract this, camp authorities used "time, tact, and personal contact" to gain trust and to "arouse confidence on the part of the Japanese prisoners of war."[25] For the most part, these initiatives were successful and the prisoners' attitudes towards the program changed for the better. But, at the end of October, Lt. Colonel Moore had to transfer a group of recalcitrant critics, including seven officers and twelve enlisted men, to Camp Hearne. The twelve enlisted men had not only disrupted work and rejected the goals of the program, but they also had formed a criminal gang. In their short time at Camp Huntsville, these men had succeeded in beating up several POWs, including an officer, before they were discovered. Their removal was a success, and a "remarkable change was observed during the short period" after they were gone. Once the various transfers were completed, 19 officers, 31 NCOs, and 136 enlisted men remained at the camp.[26]

Ideologies and Life at Camp Huntsville

The Japanese POWs who arrived at Camp Huntsville lived with values and ideologies different from their German and Italian counterparts. Many of these POWs believed that "they had turned traitor to their country and would never be able to return."[27] In Japan, guards viewed allied prisoners as the worst sort of coward. Likewise, the Japanese in Camp Huntsville and other POW camps believed that they had dishonored not only their country, but their families and themselves as well. The Japanese prisoners even refused to write letters to their families letting them know whether they were dead or alive. In their opinion, as prisoners, they were already dead.[28]

Prior to the war, Japanese General Hideki Tojo ordered the "Code of Battlefield Conduct," or the *Senjinkun*, to be given to soldiers as they prepared for battle. The book outlined behaviors expected of troops fighting under the flag of the Empire of Japan. The purpose of the *Senjinkun* was to provide soldiers with, "concrete rules of conduct, in the light of past experience, so that those in the zone of combat may wholly abide by the Imperial Rescript to enhance the moral virtues of the Imperial Army."[29] The document outlined the goals of the Imperial Army, standards of discipline, unity, aggressiveness, and the conviction to win, among other virtues.

In addition to the written mandates of the *Senjinkun*, soldiers fought for their emperor because they believed him to be descended from the heavens and god-like. All of the soldiers had been trained to believe that "the way of the subject is to be loyal to the Emperor in disregard of self, thereby supporting the Imperial Throne coextensive with the Heavens and with Earth."[30] The Emperor of Japan was a figure of political and religious importance also because he was the highest authority and head of the Shinto religion. Therefore, to die for one's country also meant to die for one's beliefs, culture, and religion.

The Japanese also held firm to their nationalistic ideals. In Japan, civilians and government officials alike considered the nation more important than the individual. The *Senjinkun* advised soldiers that "it is essential that each man, high and low, dutifully observing his place, should be determined always to sacrifice himself for the whole, in accordance with the intentions of the commander, by reposing every confidence in his comrades, and without giving even the slightest thought to personal interest and to life or death." It further advised: "The destiny of the Empire rests upon victory or defeat in battle. Do not give up under any circumstances, keeping in mind your responsibility not to tarnish the glorious history of the Imperial Army with its tradition of invincibility." Essentially, then, a soldier who surrendered or did not sacrifice his own life was a disgrace to the Japanese nation.[31]

Because all Japanese soldiers carried the *Senjinkun*, they were ingrained with the idea that the Empire of Japan expected them to fight to the death for victory. Suicide was the honorable alternative to capture or surrender. Even more acceptable was the practice of suicide, while being destructive to enemy property or personnel, such as with kamikaze attacks. The preservation of individual and collective honor prevented many Japanese soldiers from surrendering. In addition, many Japanese believed that allied captors would treat them poorly or kill them, so they avoided capture as much as possible.

Those Japanese taken prisoner were, for the most part, unconscious at the time or too badly wounded to be able to take their own lives.[32] The majority of Japanese POWs in Huntsville were members of the Navy, rather than other divisions of Japan's military force. These Japanese had been brought up to accept that Japan and the Japanese way of life was superior to all others. Therefore, when the re-education program began, many POWs were openly suspicious and hostile toward the program because they believed it to be American propaganda. Many found it difficult to become involved in the program because of "an instinctive feeling of the sanctity of matters relative to Japanese ideology." Nevertheless, the POWs reluctance to become involved in the program was eventually overcome, and many of them became more accepting of American instruction.[33]

These ideologies presented problems for the guards at Camp Huntsville. Many of them shared the ethnocentric beliefs of the white residents living in nearby Huntsville, who felt a deep resentment toward the Japanese and viewed them as racially inferior. For instance,

D.M. Phillips, president of the Huntsville-Walker County Chamber of Commerce and Commander of the local American Legion Post, responded to the end of hostilities in August 1945 by saying, "I wish they would knock a little more hell out of the Japs. For the good of the world they need to be licked some more . . . . You can't civilize or educate Germans or Japs in a short length of time." Roy Goolsby, the president of the Huntsville School Board, felt the same way, saying that the war had ended too soon. "Eventually," he said, "we will have to do the same thing to them again. They are not really whipped yet. Personally, to save the lives of thousands of American boys, I'm in favor of using gas [against the Japanese] which, though just as deadly as the atomic bomb, is more humane. [The] History of Japan show[s] that they have always been treacherous and they have no place as a nation."[34]

Prisoners and Re-education

Despite the mutual ethnocentric distortions of the other shared by both the Japanese and the Americans, the re-education program did seem to have at least some success. Shortly after the close of World War II, Moriji Yamaga, a high-ranking POW from Camp Huntsville, returned to his native Japan to find it in "miserable" condition. "I returned suddenly in January [1946]," he later wrote, and "after having been away . . . for four years and four months I could not help but be amazed." Whole neighborhoods had been destroyed, prices for food and consumer goods were grossly inflated, and the spirit of the people was broken. In response to this apocalyptic situation, Yamaga decided to publish a book based on his experience at Camp Huntsville. Titled *American Democracy and Its Ways*, this edited collection of seventeen lectures by professors at Sam Houston State Teachers College presented topics ranging from the "development of representative government" to the "expansion of American democracy" and "liberty and human rights." As editor of the text, Yamaga hoped that the book might help "reform and reestablish" his "fine and democratic country," which was "emerging from an era of militaristic dictatorship" that had destroyed the lives and livelihoods of millions of people in Japan and abroad. Yamaga was no opportunistic quisling, but, as a seasoned naval meteorologist, he gave his interrogators significant and useful details on both the Japanese and Russian militaries. His postwar embrace of liberal democracy then seemed to be a natural progression of his own personal development. At any rate, collegiate-level lectures composed

Jap Prisoners Study and Raise Gardens

Japanese prisoners of war at the Huntsville camp are being instructed in the operations of American democracy in addition to their regular duties around the camp area. In the upper photo are shown some of the group of 25 selected prisoners engaged in the educational program attending lecture being given by Dr. C. W. Hepner, a civilian who has spent 30 years in Japan. In the lower photo are shown some of the other prisoners, captured on several of the islands in the Pacific, working in a small garden at the prison. All tilling of the soil is done with shovels. The Japs are very adept at gardening.

Japanese prisoners at Camp Huntsville. Clipping from Record Group 389, Provost Marshal General's Office, Executive Division, Technical Information Officer Publicity File, 1942-1945, Food POW to Korea, Box 21, Modern Military Records Branch, National Archives, College Park, Maryland. Courtesy National Archives.

PAGE 8.

THE HUNTSVILLE ITEM

Established in 1850

"A Better Newspaper For a Greater Huntsville and Walker County"

Gulf Coast

Press

Association

MEMBER

TEXAS **PTA** PRESS

ASSOCIATION

North-East Texas

Press

Association

MRS. ROSS WOODALL and WM. R. WOODALL................Publishers
MRS. ROSS WOODALL..Editor

Entered in the postoffice every Thursday at Huntsville, Walker County, Texas, as Second-class mail matter.

PUSHOVER -- ?

So you think Japan is a pushover, eh?

Well, get a load of this.

Japan's home islands are industrialized to the last kilowatt hour, to the last rivet, to the last pair of hands of the 35 millions of Japanese. And the Japs have 400 million conquered Asiatics slaving away for her, too. Japan constitutes the second largest empire in the world today.

The Japanese losses have been small in comparison to the size of the job we must do. We haven't yet locked with the main force of the enemy. Japanese losses are not equal to the normal replacements.

Many Americans, unfortunately, have the mistaken idea that once Germany is out of the war, Japan will be a pushover. American military and naval leaders certainly don't think so.

Iwo Jima should dissipate any illusions of Japan being a pushover. Thousands of Marines died, and more thousands were put out of the fight, the worst fight in the history of the corps, and all on an island so small our Marines could shoot clear across it.

As we get closer to the heart of the Jap empire, our task is becoming harder and tougher. Our fighting men need all the support you can give them. You have a magnificent opportunity to give such support in the Mighty 7th War Loan by buying more and bigger bonds. Every American has his own personal quota. Find out what yours is — and make it.

So you think the Japs a pushover?

Tell that to the Marines.

"Pushover--?" *Huntsville Item*, May 24, 1945. Courtesy, *Huntsville Item*.

in an alien tongue were probably the least effective tools in changing hearts and minds, and officials made sure that prisoners participated in other activities besides listening to the professors.[35]

At Camp Huntsville, a daily news sheet for the prisoners to read began under the direction of the chaplain in the camp. The news not only provided relief from the day-to-day activities of the camp, but it also enabled the POWs to apply their English skills that they had learned during re-education. Japanese POWs who were members of the project selected stories from American newspapers and translated them into Japanese. At first, the newspaper was read to the prisoners, but after a time they were copied for distribution for the prisoners to read themselves. Security did not seem to be an issue with the news sheets because the translations were only checked for accuracy of the translation.[36]

The information contained in the news sheets consisted of data on Japan and the effects of the American presence in the country. One of the major stories in the news concerned the recent separation of the Shinto religion and the Japanese government, when Emperor Hirohito had rejected "his supposed divinity." The news sheet was also meant to further the re-education program's purpose. Short sketches from *Reader's Digest* and *The New York Times* were published such as the article "Have Nations Any Morals?" The selection of content in the news sheets was relegated to documents that promoted democracy or a democratic way of life, self-reliance, and any other article that would promote the rebuilding of Japan in the democratic manner. Original works produced by the prisoners themselves were also included in the news sheet such as poems, character sketches, and articles.[37]

Prisoner morale was a big factor in the success of the re-education program. Therefore, prisoners had a myriad of assorted activities to choose from in their time away from classes. Athletics was promoted through softball, table tennis, and baseball. Equipment for recreation was donated by the camp prisoner war fund, which was established on October 22, 1945. The camp fund also provided painting supplies, chalks, and colored pencils for personal art projects as well as games, carpentry tools, and theater props.[38]

In addition to arts and athletics, entertainment was provided for the POWs as well. A 16 millimeter projector and screen were received in the camp and showed "The Purple Heart" and "Guadalcanal Diary" with censorship provided by the commanding officer. Radio programs were also set to air through the camp for entertainment. On December 10, a public address system was put in place and planned to air radio programs, classical music, popular music, and music performed by the YMCA.[39]

Religious services were also offered at the camp. Although the Shinto religion had recently been divorced from the government in Japan, at Camp Huntsville the Japanese POWs were encouraged to believe that a close relationship existed between Christianity and democracy. The prisoners were not forced to attend church, but those who did were apparently impacted by the services. In fact, attendance at religious services reached a high point of forty two percent with the average attendance of about twenty five percent. The religious services offered at Camp Huntsville added to the indoctrination program in that it taught moral principles in correlation with the rights of the individual. Essentially, all extracurricular activities aimed to emphasize the lessons taught to the POWs during their scheduled re-education.[40]

While athletics and arts took up hours in the day, not all prisoners were interested in such pursuits. A growing number of POWs expressed their desire to earn wages so that they could take advantage of the camp canteen. On September 21, the Special Projects Division, under the command of Lieutenant Colonel Edward Davison, authorized "the payment of wages and the granting of privileges to the Japanese prisoners of war in the form of extra canteen items, clothing and food."[41] The approved labor opportunities began on a trial basis. By October, two groups of fifteen men started working on local farms for 25 cents an hour with a maximum of an eight-hour workday.[42] It was hoped that if the trial period met with success, then the number of laborers would grow to between thirty and fifty POWs.

There were virtually no problems in the labor area, and the civilian supervisors who oversaw the POWs were "satisfied with the work of the prisoners of war in the various maintenance installations and in the camp."[43] One incident involved four POWs who failed to report for afternoon labor duty, having already worked during the morning hours. This was the exception rather than the rule, however, as most prisoners were willing to work so that they could spend their earnings on extra comforts from the canteen. Indeed, the camp chaplain reported that "the prisoners all wish to work as much as possible and plenty of work heightens their morale."[44] Higher morale meant a more willing attitude toward the re-education program as a whole.

There were a small number of jobs available in the camp as firefighters, orderlies, gardeners in the camp vegetable farm, and cooks and laborers in the mess hall. Also available was work in the camp canteen, camp stockade, medical department, and other various projects around the camp such as maintenance work. However, these jobs could only employ around 50 men due to the smaller workload at the camp. Therefore, the military arranged labor opportunities through outside sources as they had with the German POWs. The majority of the contracted labor performed by the Japanese POWs was agricultural.[45]

Eventually, camp officials abolished the eight-hour workday in favor of a workday of four to six hours. An easier workday benefited both the prisoners and those running the camp as a lighter load guaranteed that the POWs were not overworked and therefore more open to instruction and indoctrination. A prisoner's workload lightened even more if they expressed further interest in the program outside of regular studies. This shortened workday allocated two and a half hours for class, an extra hour for the study of English, and during the last month an hour for the study of American literature. The Japanese POWs worked a total of 16,430 hours from September until December.[46]

The End of the War and the Closing of Camp Huntsville

World War II ended on September 2, 1945, when Japan officially surrendered aboard the *USS Missouri*. The close of the war did not, however, result in the immediate freedom or repatriation of the POWs. Although most Japanese prisoners in the United States were sent home by October 1945, the men who came to Camp Huntsville remained for a few months longer to participate in the re-education program. In fact, the end of the war may have made the program more feasible, since government officials no longer entertained any serious concerns about the indoctrination program violating the Geneva Convention of 1929.[47]

Camp Huntsville remained functioning until its deactivation in January 1946, when the indoctrination program also ended. There were several reasons for this abrupt shut down. To begin with, General Douglas MacArthur believed that indoctrination would be more productive on Japanese soil during the occupation of Japan. MacArthur argued that introducing Japanese civilians to the program would be, "more valuable than a less concentrated program with fewer personal contacts."[48] MacArthur's word carried much weight in Washington, and he had considerable support from other officials and academics who had studied the issue. Thus, the re-education efforts were promptly relocated to Japan.

Once word of the program's closing arrived at the camp, the staff delivered two last lectures, which reiterated the need for democracy in Japan and the broader world. The success of these last two classes or of the re-education program in general, is unknown, as a follow-up study was never performed on the Japanese POWs. The short amount of time devoted to the project and the failure to collect proper documentation on the effort make it difficult to assess the program. At any rate, on December 26, 1945, the Special Projects Division sent word to Camp Huntsville that the POWs should prepare for repatriation to Japan. By January 5, 1946, Camp Huntsville was officially deactivated.[49]

CHAPTER VI. COUNTRY CAMPUS AND THE POST-WAR ERA

With Carolyn Carroll and Amy Hyden

Acquiring the Land

After Camp Huntsville closed in 1946, the land and buildings sat idle, while the government decided how best to dispense with the property. An opportunity soon presented itself as U.S. veterans returned home. During World War II, few houses and apartments had been constructed in Huntsville, and now the returning war veterans, who enjoyed the benefits of the GI Bill of Rights, needed campus housing. Many veterans took advantage of the financial assistance for higher education and training through the GI Bill, and by the summer of 1946, 521 veterans had enrolled at Sam Houston State Teachers College (SHSTC). With limited housing available, landlords in Huntsville exacerbated the housing crisis by increasing rents. Veterans even considered pitching tents. Sam Houston Veterans Club president Bill Thielen pleaded with landlords to lower rents. Options were discussed locally to settle housing issues, but to no avail, resulting in federal intervention. U.S. Senator Tom Connally and Representative Tom Pickett introduced a rent control act, which passed and became law in October 1946. Though this act helped veterans and students obtain more affordable housing, there still was not enough to go around. The shortage prompted D.C. Holleman, the business manager of SHSTC, to encourage the president of the college, Dr. Harmon Lowman, to pursue acquisition of the former POW camp. The abandoned camp provided the ideal solution to ease the housing crisis for students, faculty, and administrators.[1]

The War Assets Corporation built the POW camp at a cost of three million dollars, but placed it for sale at an asking price of six hundred thousand dollars. Desperately needing this facility, but unable to obtain the funds to purchase it, Dr. Lowman addressed a letter to the president of the board of directors of the War Assets Corporation requesting that it be deeded to SHSTC at no cost. Lowman pleaded his case for the facility and stressed the national benefits that would accrue from the transaction. After several meetings, the agreed purchase price came to $1.00. The United States Government, through the War Assets Corporation, conveyed to SHSTC 833.49 acres of land and 405 buildings for educational use. Sam Houston State Teachers College took possession of the personal and real property of the camp in June 1946.[2] The deed specified that for the first five years from the date of conveyance, the land could only be used for health and educational purposes. College administrators filed semi-annual reports with the War Assets Corporation or its successor on the utilization of the property. If found in violation of the deed, ownership of all personal and real property would revert back to the United States government. In 1949, the Department of Health, Education, and Welfare became the government's overseer and enforcer of the deed restrictions. The acting regional property coordinator wrote a letter in 1956 to President Lowman requesting an update on property use to ensure SHSTC compliance. Lowman curtly responded in writing with one sentence and a copy of the deed, politely telling the agency that it was well beyond the five-year restriction period. By that time, SHSTC could use the property as it deemed fit.[3]

Building, Renovation, and Occupation

Following the purchase of the camp, President Lowman secured $200,000 to fund renovations at the site, and he expected another $320,000 in the months to follow. These monies were appropriated in order to renovate 133 buildings, which would provide living quarters for eleven hundred students. In addition, the school constructed a twelve-acre athletic field and artificial lake for recreational purposes, and repaired the stables for a riding academy and small arms range.[4]

Anticipating an increase in enrollment at SHSTC, administrators launched an advertising campaign informing prospective students of the new branch facility and affordable housing. Since rent was one of the college's main sources of revenue, rates were set with this in mind. An advisor from the investment securities firm who issued some of the bond monies for the housing project wrote President Lowman in August of 1946 suggesting what rates to charge. He reminded Lowman that, because of the housing crisis, only an exterior facelift and not a full-scale renovation of the barracks should take place. He

"Thank You," *Huntsville Item*, August 16, 1945. Courtesy, *Huntsville Item*.

felt that rent should be lower than what was charged on the main campus, given the fact that SHSTC's new Country Campus was ten miles out of town, and the facilities were substandard. The cost for on-campus room and board in the 1946-47 school year was $180 per semester, and approved off-campus housing ran from $25-$35 per month. Keeping this in mind, he suggested $7.00 a month for single dorm space. He also addressed his concerns that converting some of the barracks into apartments would not be cost efficient; however, Lowman envisioned a future for Country Campus beyond the immediate need and proceeded to construct apartments.[5]

Apartments rented for $25.00 to $32.00 a month, depending upon the number of bedrooms. Students had an option of paying $20.00 a month and making up the difference by working one hour a day at the campus. The rent for a single student in a dorm room was $8.00 a month.[6] One advertisement boasted of country club living when, in truth, most of the buildings were wood and tarpaper structures in need of plumbing. Many students soon learned the hard way that the new camp was a work in progress.[7]

The fall enrollment at SHSTC in 1946 broke all previous records, confirming the administration's predictions. A total of 952 veterans enrolled at the college, and as early as August 1946, faculty and administrators began moving to Country Campus. Dr. and Mrs. Lowman were among the first to move, occupying the former home of the commander of the POW camp. Dean James G. Gee and his wife moved into what was part of the POW Hospital; Professor Everett Frasier and family resided in the former dental building; and E. C. Watkins and his wife resided in the former telephone exchange building. Every building on the campus was transformed into useable space.[8] By October 1946, Country Campus housed 56 married couples, 150 single men, and 34 single women. The former POW barracks were converted into apartments for single men and married couples, and the POW hospital was converted into a women's dorm. As remodeling at Country Campus continued to progress, this branch of SHSTC began to form a close-knit community of students, faculty, and administrators.[9]

The campus improvement projects continued and by February 1947, a crew of 98 construction workers, including fourteen students, completed 16 of the projected 160 apartments. The plan was to convert 40 of the old POW barracks into apartments, each with four units thus allowing for the accommodation of at least four hundred people. President Lowman wanted student involvement in the improvement phases so he devised a plan to hire student contractors.

Map of Country Campus.

Each of these students would hire a crew and make sure that jobs were finished in a timely manner. Lowman paid students by the completed barrack rather than by an hourly wage.[10] By July 1, 1948, construction was underway to convert twenty two addtional bedroom apartments before the start of the fall semester.[11] By October of that year, several hundred residents lived at Country Campus, including thirty faculty, more than 180 single men, and at least 290 in married housing. For married couples with or without children, apartment rent increased to $35 a month, with utilities and bus transportation to and from town included. For single men, the cost of room and board was $30 a month. The apartments were equipped with moderate furnishings, like a gas stove and ice box. Occupants were to furnish accessories. The apartments were clean and designed to be comfortable, but in no way were they similar in comfort and quality to the housing in town. As one couple aptly put it, "The apartments are not what we would want to live in the remainder of our lives, but they are better than the average apartment you can get these days." The population boom in 1948 made Country Campus the second largest town in Walker County.[12]

Campus Life

Life at Country Campus resembled small town living. Inhabitants enjoyed the benefits of a commissary, library, fire station, post office, laundry, bakery, outdoor activities, and a self-sustaining water system. Buses were provided for students and faculty needing transportation to the main campus, and the younger children living at Country Campus attended elementary school in the nearby town of Riverside. In November 1946, forty-five veterans organized the Thompson-Knight Post of the American Legion at the campus. The name of the Post honored Ray Seale Thompson of Leona, Texas, and Roland Knight of Centerville, Texas, both were SHSTC students killed in action during World War II. In December 1946, the former officers club of the POW camp transformed into the student union building, which hosted an array of activities including weekly dances. One night each week students would pay twenty-five cents per ticket to gather to dance from 8:00-10:00 p.m. with music provided by local artists.[13]

The community published its own newspaper, the *Country Campus News*, keeping the inhabitants informed about current events

Entrance to Country Campus. Courtesy, Thomason Room, Newton Gresham Library, Sam Houston State University.

Faculty apartment at Country Campus. Courtesy, Thomason Room, Newton Gresham Library, Sam Houston State University.

in the community and at SHSTC. A few salvaged editions of the *Country Campus Journal* from July 1 to August 30, 1948 give a glimpse of residential life on the campus. The paper ran when school was in session, so these publications span the summer semester. The exciting news of the summer seemed to be the impending opening of the post office, scheduled for August 1, 1948. The population at the camp that summer was the highest ever at 769. Two hundred and five of those residents were under the age of five. Interestingly, there was enough to keep smaller children busy. Country Campus boasted a baseball team that played all over the area from Elkhart to Tomball, and there were tennis courts, and a movie theater. To combat the ever-present Texas heat, the fire department filled the drainage ditch three nights a week, turning it into a splash pool. Residents were warned, however, to be careful when out at night as roaming dogs were a growing problem. An announcement in the *Campus Journal* informed owners that dogs would be shot on sight if they lacked a rabies tag.[14]

For those living at Country Campus, the student union building was their connection to the main campus. Feeling that they were just as much a part of SHSTC as those living in Huntsville, many Country Campus students became disgruntled with the fact that they could not participate in student council activities. In November 1950, eighty-one Country Campus students signed a petition in an attempt to place a representative with voting privileges on the council. The petition met with approval and was brought before the college assembly for a vote.[15]

For the most part, Country Campus students wanted inclusion in all activities that the main campus held. Occasionally, however, special events were held at Country Campus. For instance, over the Christmas Holiday in 1950, a reunion of the original County Campus pioneers took place. Stories and memories were shared, and the highlight of the evening was the presentation of Frances Bowers' Master's research titled "The History of Country Campus." Unfortunately, due to illness, the Bowers were not able to attend, so Mr. Sheldon Fisher read the paper to the group.[16] Country Campus students also wanted to form their own Future Farmers of American (FFA) chapter. In September 1950, they broke away from the main campus' town chapter, but by February 1951 dwindling membership at the County Campus chapter resulted in its closing.[17]

Baseball

In April 1947, the construction of a new baseball field came to completion. The complex not only hosted SHSTC's games but also became a prime spring training location for the farm clubs of professional baseball teams such as the Pittsburgh Pirates and Chicago Cubs.[18] Cuba's professional baseball league entertained the possibilities of using the Country Campus setup as a spring training site for their farm clubs. In addition to the professionals, many area high school baseball teams trained at the field. Known as the Lone Star Baseball Camp, this facility put SHSTC and Huntsville in the national limelight by drawing in not just local high school students but youths from all over the United States.[19] Every spring, Country Campus would host a scholarship camp for high school and Jr. College baseball stars charging them $1.00 a day for room and board. Many major league scouts traveled from Kansas City, New York, Chicago, and Detroit to attend the camp.[20] In January 1955, the Pittsburgh Pirates' management considered sending their farm club to another site for spring training. President Lowman had big plans for Country Campus, and Pittsburgh's planned move threatened to have a negative impact. Therefore, to entice Pittsburgh's farm club to attend training at County Campus, he added a physical therapy area for the pitchers. Lowman's incentives worked. The farm club, comprised of four hundred players from Montana, Arizona, California, Pennsylvania, Texas, and Kansas arrived in March 1955, making it one of the largest minor league training camps in the Pittsburgh organization.[21]

Academics and the Josey School

As Country Campus grew, SHSTC administrators began to focus on the construction of the branch department that would be independent of the main campus. Administration buildings, classrooms, and housing facilities, were needed on the site. In December 1946, officials announced that construction of the SHSTC branch college would begin immediately, ultimately providing classrooms to accommodate at least a thousand students. The initial desire for the branch campus was that students could take traditional college courses alongside vocational training courses. Core college courses such as science, English, art, and education were offered from the outset, but in May 1947, State Representative M. B. Etheredge witnessed Texas Governor Beauford Jester sign HB 471, making the Josey School of Vocational Education another recognized branch of SHSTC. The school offered a two-year training schedule in vocational education and did not require trainees to qualify for college entrance, thus opening the doors to many returning veterans.[22] Although, most of the Josey School was housed on the main campus, the students also took classes and lived at Country Campus, thus completing the desire by President Lowman to have a variety of courses offered at the branch facility. By 1952, Country Campus boasted three hundred furnished apartments to house students in the Josey School.[23] The two-year program was ideal for veterans needing to obtain critical skills as they transitioned back to civilian life. Beyond simple vocational training, the men enrolled at the school were primed to become small business owners. Not only did the men receive trade certificates, college administrators implemented a plan where some vocational students also earned valuable college credits to apply towards a future degree.[24] President Lowman wanted this school to benefit both male and female veterans. In 1948, Lowman corresponded with Lt. Col. Mary Agnes Brown, who was the officer in charge of the Women's

Army Corps (WAC) veterans. In this letter, he informed her that the vocational school had a department of distributive education which he thought would be of particular value to WAC veterans. He then asked if it was possible to obtain the names and addresses of the WAC veterans who lived in the Southwestern states so that he could call their attention to the opportunities for training at the Josey School. The goal of the Josey School was for students to learn both the how and the why behind business practices.[25]

The campus as a whole benefitted from the different vocational trades taught. For instance, students in the meat cutter's trade worked with poultry, sheep, pork, and beef. They learned how to make cuts of meat and prepare them for frozen storage. The slaughterhouse located at Country Campus provided meat to the general store to sell to residents at a much lower cost than other markets. When the general store closed, not only did patrons have to pay higher prices for meat. but the quality was lacking. Another contribution from the men at the Josey School came when they joined forces with the college's Industrial Arts Department headed by J. B. Snodgrass to build a house for the Huntsville Girl Scouts Association. In addition, a talented

Lowman Hall at Country Campus. Courtesy, Thomason Room, Newton Gresham Library, Sam Houston State University.

auto mechanic student, Johnnie Vester Wisc, made a tractor from scratch. He used various parts from different makes and models.[26]

Other college departments also contributed to the good of the community. The agricultural department utilized the land at Country Campus to support a program that highlighted the way different grass seeds and legumes improved pastures for cattle grazing. The students provided public demonstrations to area ranchers showing them how green and healthy pastures resulted in better meat quality. Livestock was not the department's only focus; professors also implemented plans for soil conservation. The program was successful, and residents at Country Campus planted crops for their own use and for the community. [27]

Closing Country Campus

When Country Campus opened to residents in 1946, President Lowman envisioned grand possibilities for the site. The 1948-1949 daily schedule for the college listed forty-one classes, from English literature to agriculture that were taught on-site at Country Campus. The very next year, that number shrank to twenty-nine, and by the

In the garden at Country Campus. Courtesy, Thomason Room, Newton Gresham Library, Sam Houston State University.

Student apartment at Country Campus. Courtesy, Thomason Room, Newton Gresham Library, Sam Houston State University.

time of publication for the 1952-53 school year, only eight course offerings remained. Most of those classes focused on agriculture, but the golf classes were also held at the Country Campus course.[23]

By the early 1950s, enrollment at the college and the Josey School began to decline. The 1952 summer session at the Josey School totaled only 56 men of which nine were visitors, and President Lowman feared a further decrease in the fall. Enrollment records for the previous year totaled 125 students. Newly elected Regent John C. Calhoun toured SHSTC campuses and seemed deeply interested in the Josey School stating, "The vocational end of education is equally as important as the academic." Apparently his words were not enough because a 30% across-the-board budget cut at SHSTC implemented by the College's Board of Regents in the fall of 1951 greatly affected Country Campus. In addition to budget cuts, the Veterans' Adjustment Act of 1952 also decreased benefits for higher education. Under this Act, the government no longer paid tuition directly to colleges and universities, but instead gave each veteran a flat monthly fee of approximately $110.00 to apply towards educational expenses. "The number of WWII veterans [was]decreasing each year at SHSTC," the registrar at the time declared. "The veterans who were planning on finishing college are through by now and the remaining veterans are under the new GI Bill."[29]

During the period of 1955-1959, overall enrollment at SHSTC began to steadily climb, renewing hope that Country Campus would remain a viable asset. To accommodate the college's growth spurt, improvements to the main campus increased. Construction commenced on a new student union building, replacing the one at Country Campus. In addition, the main campus witnessed a flurry of development, including the Farrington Science Building, the Evans Building for the English Department, and the Haley Building for the Home Economics and Biology departments.

In 1956, President Lowman and the Board of Regents compiled a twenty-year plan for the future development of SHSTC. The goal was to make the main campus for students in their first two years of college work. At Country Campus, the school would offer the last two years of undergraduate work, leading to a bachelor's degree, and graduate work, leading to a master's or doctoral degree. SHSTC at this time was one of the largest teachers' colleges in America, and the Regents felt Country Campus was the ideal location for new expansion capable of accommodating five thousand students. Lowman predicted that over the course of this twenty-year plan, thirty-two million dollars would be made available to build the new college at Country Campus. For numerous reasons, however, political and financial pressures led not to the growth but to the decline of Country Campus. Academic instruction at the site ended in the late 1950s, and the administration started to slowly sell off or relocate the buildings and personal property.[30]

Country Campus Today

By the late 1960s, devoid of daily activity or permanent residents, Country Campus became an eyesore. Accordingly, in June 1971, Sam Houston State University (SHSU) launched a large-scale cleanup of the site. Led by Dr. Frank Leathers, the financial vice-president of the university, the remaining vacated buildings were sold and the concrete foundations leveled. The university doubled the size of the golf course at this time, extending it all the way to Highway 19. The agriculture department still utilized the land for livestock raising and shop purposes, so two new metal buildings were erected to accommodate these projects. The only residents of Country Campus were a few caretakers, whose houses were left standing. Later, in the mid-1980s, Delta Tau Alpha, the agriculture honor society, posted a new sign on Highway 19, marking the entrance to Country Campus, which had largely been forgotten by the students at Sam Houston State University.[31]

When Dr. Lowman ushered in several years of progress and building projects in the late 1950s, the university planned for and placed a telescope on top of the newly completed Farrington Science building. In 1958, when the project began, there was little in the way of light pollution on and around campus, but by 1985 the telescope was rendered useless due to the increase in lighting on the main campus. Backed by the university, the science department moved the telescope to Country Campus where they built a proper observatory to house the apparatus. In 1986, Rice University entered into negotiations with SHSU to partner with them on the telescope project, but by early 1987 they secured funds for their own telescope in Sugar Land, Texas. At this time, Sam Houston University had the fourth best telescope in the state.

Stargazing became increasingly popular among students and faculty. In the early 1990s, Professor Frank Cooper held "star parties" at Country Campus for his students, but local residents and other faculty were always welcome.[32] In 1993, Sam Dominey, distinguished alumnus, Country Campus resident, and son of one of the original landowners, purchased Country Campus from Sam Houston State University. He converted most of the land back to its pre-war pasture status, but he kept the golf course and the observatory. Dominey deeded 1.96 acres of land back to the university in 1997 for a permanent observatory location.[33] Shortly after the deed was complete, the physics department began construction on a new observatory that housed twenty-four, eighteen, and eight-inch telescopes. The old observatory was also moved to the site and housed a sixteen-inch Meade telescope for research purposes. The observatory is still used by the Physics department to the present day.[34]

Though most of the land at Country Campus reverted back to its original form when it was purchased in 1993, local community leaders strove to keep the images and purpose of the POW internment camp and Country Campus alive. On April 27, 2007, an official Texas historical marker was unveiled at the site. Walker County Judge Robert D. Pierce welcomed guests to the dedication ceremony and acknowledged those responsible for making Camp

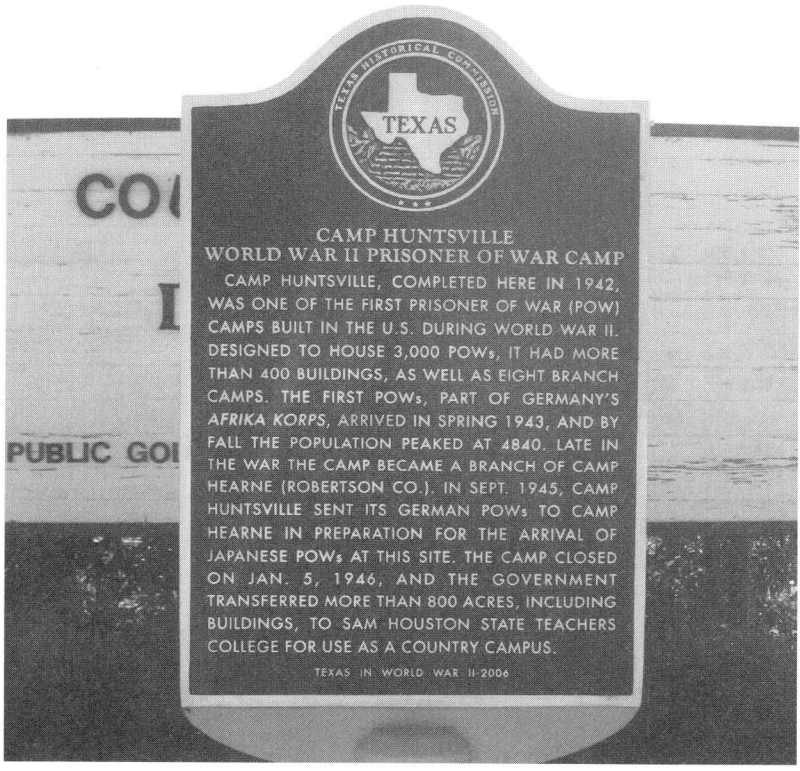

Historical Marker for Camp Huntsville.

Huntsville a state-sanctioned historical site. The honored parties included military historian William A. McWhorter, chair of the Walker County Historical Commission James D. Patton, and vice chair Donna Coffen whose mother was a civilian worker at the camp.[35]

Conclusion

In late May 1979, Karl Heinz Blumenthal, then 56, returned to the remnants of Camp Huntsville for the first time since the end of World War II. In 1942, Blumenthal had been a 20-year-old German soldier in General Rommel's *Afrika Korps* captured by Allied forces and brought to Texas via New York City. The very first days of his captivity could not have been very pleasant in that the prisoners in their soiled and torn combat fatigues had to march at least three miles from their last train station in Riverside to the internment facilities. But things certainly got better for Blumenthal and his peers once they got to the actual camp. "We had a wonderful time," Blumenthal gushed. He marveled that the prisoners actually got paid for their work, and he revealed that spartan punishments of bread and water for misbehavior were generally commuted to a single day. Blumenthal's experiences were not unusual: "the enemy within was never without." It is a tribute, then, to the character of the Americans of the greatest generation that they treated even the most despicable Nazis with respect and mercy. In fact, even their re-education efforts, however illegal in a technical sense, were done without violent coercion. It should not surprise us then that after the war as veterans returned home, they entered the very buildings that had once held prisoners of war and took up books to study the history of democracy and its implications for the future. This was indeed the era of idealism and the hubris that set U.S. policy for the remainder of the American century.

The hospital building at Camp Huntsville as it looks today. Courtesy, Jeffrey L. Littlejohn.

APPENDIX. THE GENEVA CONVENTION OF JULY 27, 1929 RELATIVE TO THE TREATMENT OF PRISONERS OF WAR

Convention between the United States of America and other powers, relating to prisoners of war. Signed at Geneva, July 27, 1929; ratification advised by the Senate, January 7, 1932; ratified by the President, January 16, 1932, ratification of the United States of America deposited with the Government of Switzerland, February 4, 1932; proclaimed, August 4, 1932.

BY THE PRESIDENT OF THE UNITED STATES OF AMERICA

A PROCLAMATION

WHEREAS, a Convention Relating to the Treatment of Prisoners of War was signed by the respective Plenipotentiaries of the United States of America and forty-six other countries, at Geneva on July 27, 1929 the original of which Convention in the French language is word for word as follows:

Translation

CONVENTION OF JULY 27, 1929, RELATIVE TO THE TREATMENT OF PRISONERS OF WAR.

The President of the German Reich, the President of the United States of America, the Federal President of the Republic of Austria, His Majesty the King of the Belgians, the President of the Republic of Bolivia, the President of the Republic of the United States of Brazil, His Majesty the King of Great Britain, Ireland, and the British Dominions beyond the Seas, Emperor of India, His Majesty the King of the Bulgarians, the President of the Republic of Chile, the President of the Republic of China, the President of the Republic of Colombia, the President of the Republic of Cuba, His Majesty the King of Denmark and Iceland, the President of the Dominican Republic, His Majesty the King of Egypt, His Majesty the King of Spain, the President of the Republic of Estonia, the President of the Republic of Finland, the President of the French Republic, the President of the Hellenic Republic, His Serene Highness the Regent of Hungary, His Majesty the King of Italy, His Majesty the Emperor of Japan, the President of the Republic of Latvia, Her Royal Highness the Grand Duchess of Luxembourg, the President of the United States of Mexico, the President of the Republic of Nicaragua, His Majesty the King of Norway, Her Majesty the Queen of the Netherlands, His Imperial Majesty the Shah of Persia the President of the Republic of Poland, the President of the

Portuguese Republic, His Majesty the King of Rumania, His Majesty the King of the Serbs, Croats and Slovenes, His Majesty the King of Siam, His Majesty the King of Sweden, the Swiss Federal Council, the President of the Czechoslovak Republic, the President of the Turkish Republic, the President of the Oriental Republic of Uruguay, [and] the President of the Republic of the United States of Venezuela, recognizing that, in the extreme case of a war, it will be the duty of every Power to diminish, so far as possible the unavoidable rigors thereof an to mitigate the fate of prisoners of war; desirous of developing the principles which inspired the international conventions of The Hague, in particular the Convention relative to the laws and customs of war and the Regulations annexed thereto; have decided to conclude a Convention to that end.

TITLE I. GENERAL PROVISIONS.

ARTICLE 1.

The present Convention shall apply, without prejudice to the stipulations of Title VII:
1) To all persons mentioned in Articles 1, 2 and 3 of the Regulations annexed to the Hague Convention respecting the laws and customs of war on land, of October 18, 1907, and captured by the enemy.

2) To all persons belonging to the armed forces of belligerent parties, captured by the enemy in the course of military operations at sea or in the air, except for such derogations as might be rendered inevitable by the conditions of capture. However, such derogations shall not infringe upon the fundamental principles of the present Convention; they shall cease from the moment when the persons captured have rejoined a prisoners-of-war camp.

ARTICLE 2.

Prisoners of war are in the power of the hostile Power, but not of the individuals or corps who have captured them.

They must at all times be humanely treated and protected, particularly against acts of violence, insults and public curiosity.

Measures of reprisal against them are prohibited.

ARTICLE 3.

Prisoners of war have the right to have their person and their honor respected. Women shall be treated with all the regard due to their sex.
Prisoners retain their full civil status.

ARTICLE 4.

The Power detaining prisoners of war is bound to provide for their maintenance.

Difference in treatment among prisoners is lawful only when it is based on the military rank, state of physical or mental health, professional qualifications or sex of those who profit thereby.

TITLE II. CAPTURE.

ARTICLE 5.

Every prisoner of war is bound to give, if he is questioned on the subject, his true name and rank, or else his regimental number.

If he infringes this rule, he is liable to have the advantages given to prisoners of his class curtailed.

No coercion may be used on prisoners to secure information as to the condition of their army or country. Prisoners who refuse to answer may not be threatened, insulted, or exposed to unpleasant or disadvantageous treatment of any kind whatever.

If, because of his physical or mental condition, a prisoner is unable to identify himself, he shall be turned over to the medical corps.

ARTICLE 6.

All effects and objects of personal use except arms, horses, military equipment and military papers shall remain in the possession of prisoners of war, as well as metal helmets and gas masks.

Money in the possession of prisoners may not be taken away from them except by order of an officer and after the amount is determined. A receipt shall be given. Money thus taken away shall be entered to the amount of each prisoner.

Identification documents, insignia of rank, decorations and objects of value may not be taken from prisoners.

TITLE III. CAPTIVITY.

SECTION I. EVACUATION OF PRISONERS OF WAR.

ARTICLE 7.

Prisoners of war shall be evacuated within the shortest possible period after their capture, to spots located in a region far enough from the zone of combat for them to be out of danger.

Only prisoners who, because of wounds or sickness would run greater risks by being evacuated than by remaining where they are may be temporarily kept in a dangerous zone.

Prisoners shall not be needlessly exposed to danger while awaiting their evacuation from the combat zone.

Evacuation of prisoners on foot may normally be effected only by stages of 20 kilometers a day, unless the necessity of reaching water and food depots requires longer stages.

ARTICLE 8.

Belligerents axe bound mutually to notify each other of their capture of prisoners within the shortest period possible, through the intermediary of the information bureaus, such as are organized according to Article 77. They are likewise bound to inform each other of the official addresses to which the correspondence of their families may be sent to prisoners of war.

As soon as possible, every prisoner must be enabled to correspond with his family himself, under the conditions provided in Articles 36 et seq.

As regards prisoners captured at sea, the provisions of the present article shall be observed as soon as possible after arrival at port.

SECTION II. PRISONERS-OF-WAR CAMPS.

ARTICLE 9.

Prisoners of war may be interned in a town, fortress, or other place, and bound not to go beyond certain fixed limits. They may also be interned in enclosed camps; they may not be confined or imprisoned except as an indispensable measure of safety or sanitation, and only while the circumstances which necessitate the measure continue to exist.

Prisoners captured in unhealthful regions or where the climate is injurious for persons coming from temperate regions, shall be transported, as soon as possible, to a more favorable climate.

Belligerents shall, so far as possible, avoid assembling in a single camp prisoners of different races or nationalities.

No prisoner may, at any time, be sent into a region where he might be exposed to the fire of the combat zone, nor used to give protection from bombardment to certain points or certain regions by his presence.

CHAPTER 1. Installation of Camps.

ARTICLE 10.

Prisoners of war shall be lodged in buildings or in barracks affording all possible guarantees of hygiene and healthfulness.

The quarters must be fully protected from. dampness, sufficiently heated and lighted. All precautions must be taken agains: danger of fire.

With regard to dormitories the total surface, minimum cubic amount of air, arrangement and material of bedding-the conditions shall be the same as for the troops at base camps of the detaining Power.

CHAPTER 2. Food and Clothing of Prisoners of War.

ARTICLE 11.

The food ration of prisoners of war shall be equal in quantity and quality to that of troops at base camps.

Furthermore, prisoners shall receive facilities for preparing, themselves, additional food which thy might have.

Sufficiency of potable water shall be furnished them. The use of tobacco shall be permitted. Prisoners may be employed in the kitchens.

All collective disciplinary measures affecting the food are prohibited.

ARTICLE 12.

Clothing, linen and footwear shall be furnished prisoners of war by the detaining Power. Replacement and repairing of these effects must be assured regularly. In addition, laborers must receive work clothes wherever the nature of the work requires it.

Canteens shall be installed in all camps where prisoners may obtain, at the local market price, food products and ordinary objects.

Profits made by the canteens for camp administrations shall be used for the benefit of prisoners.

CHAPTER 3. Sanitary Service in Camps.

ARTICLE 13.

Belligerents shall. be bound to take all sanitary measures necessary to assure the cleanliness and healthfulness of camps and to prevent epidemics.

Prisoners of war shall have at their disposal, day and night, installations conforming to sanitary rules and constantly maintained in a state of cleanliness.

Furthermore, and without Prejudice to baths and showers of which the camp shall be as well provided as possible, prisoners shall be furnished a sufficient quantity of water for the care of their own bodily cleanliness.

It shall be possible for them to take physical exercise and enjoy the open air.

ARTICLE 14.

Every camp shall have an infirmary, where prisoners of war shall receive every kind of attention they need. If necessary, isolated quarters shall be reserved for the sick affected with contagious diseases.

Expenses of treatment, including therein those of temporary prosthetic equipment, shall become by the detaining Power.

Upon request, belligerents shall be bound to deliver to every prisoner treated an official statement showing the nature and duration of his illness as well as the attention received.

It shall be lawful for belligerents reciprocally to authorize, by means of private arrangements the retention in the camps of physicians and attendants to care for prisoners of their own country.

Prisoners affected. with a serious illness or whose condition necessitates an important surgical operation, must be admitted, at the expense of the detaining Power, to any military or civil medical unit qualified to treat them.

ARTICLE 15.

Medical inspections of prisoners of war shall be arranged at least once a month. Their purpose shall be the supervision of the general state of health and cleanliness, and the detection of contagious diseases, particularly tuberculosis and venereal diseases.

CHAPTER 4. Intellectual and Moral Needs of Prisoners of War.

ARTICLE 16

Prisoners of war shall enjoy complete liberty in the exercise of their religion, including attendance at the services of their faith, on the sole condition that they comply with the measures of order and police issued by the military authorities.

Ministers of a religion, prisoners of war, whatever their denomination, shall be allowed to minister fully to members of the same religion.

ARTICLE 17.

So far as possible belligerents shall encourage intellectual diversions and sports organized by prisoners of war.

CHAPTER 5. Internal Discipline of Camps.

ARTICLE 18.

Every camp of prisoners of war shall be placed under the command of a responsible officer.

Besides the external marks of respect provided by the regulations in force in their armies with regard to their nationals prisoners of war must salute all officers of the detaining Power.

Officers who are prisoners of war are bound to salute only officers of a higher or equal rank of that Power.

ARTICLE 19.

The wearing of insignia of rank and of decorations shall be permitted.

ARTICLE 20.

Regulations, orders, notices and proclamations of every kind must be communicated to prisoners of war in a language which they understand. The same principle shall be applied in examinations.

CHAPTER 6. Special Provisions Regarding Officers and Persons of Equivalent status. ARTICLE 21.

Upon the beginning of hostilities, belligerents shall be bound to communicate to one another the titles and ranks in use in their respective armies, with a view to assuring equality of treatment between corresponding ranks of officers and persons of equivalent status.

Officers and persons of equivalent status who are prisoners of war shall be treated with the regard due their rank and age.

ARTICLE 22.

In order to assure service in officers' camps, soldiers of the same army who are prisoners of war and, wherever possible, who speak the same language, shall be assigned thereto, in sufficient numbers, considering the rank of the officers and persons of equivalent status.

The latter shall secure their food and clothing from the pay which shall be granted them by the detaining Power. Administration of the mess-fund by the officers themselves must be facilitated in every way.

CHAPTER 7. Financial Resources of Prisoners of War.

ARTICLE 23.

Subject to private arrangements between belligerent Powers, and particularly those provided in Article 24, officers and persons of equivalent status who are prisoners of war shall receive from the detaining Power the same pay as officers of corresponding rank in the armies of that Power, on the condition, however, that this pay does not exceed that to which they are entitled in the armies of the country which they have Served. This pay shall be granted them in full, once a month if possible, and without being liable to any deduction for expenses incumbent on the detaining Power, even when they are in favor of the prisoners.

An agreement between the belligerents shall fix the rate of exchange applicable to this payment; in the absence of such an agreement, the rate adopted shall be that in force at the opening of hostilities.

All payments made to prisoners of war as pay must be reimbursed, at the end of hostilities, by the Power which they have served.

ARTICLE 24.

Upon the outbreak of hostilities, the belligerents shall, by common agreement, fix the maximum amount of ready money which prisoners of war of various ranks and classes shall be allowed to keep in their possession. Any surplus taken or withheld from a prisoner shall be entered to his account, the same as any deposit of money effected by him, and may not be converted into another currency without his consent.

Pay to the credit of their accounts shall be given to prisoners of war at the end of their captivity.

During their imprisonment, facilities shall be granted them for the transfer of these amounts, in whole or in part, to banks or private persons in their country of origin.

CHAPTER 8. Transfer of Prisoners of War.

ARTICLE 25.

Unless the conduct of military operation so requires, sick and wounded prisoners of war shall, not be transferred as long as their recovery might be endangered by the trip.

ARTICLE 26.

In case of transfer, prisoners of war shall be officially notified of their new destination in advance; they shall, be allowed to take with them their personal effects, their correspondence and packages which have arrived for them.

All due measures shall be taken that Correspondence and packages addressed to their former camp may be forwarded to them without delay.

Money deposited to the account of transferred prisoners shall be transmitted to the competent authority of their new place of residence.

The expenses occasioned by the transfer shall be charged to the detaining Power.

SECTION III. LABOR OF PRISONERS OF WAR.

CHAPTER 1. Generalities.

ARTICLE 27.

Belligerents May Utilize the labor of able prisoners of war, according to their rank and aptitude, officers and persons of equivalent status excepted.

However, if officers or persons of equivalent status request suitable work, it shall be secured for them so far as is possible,
Noncommissioned officers who are prisoners of war shall only be required to do supervisory work, unless they expressly request a remunerative occupation.

Belligerents shall be bound, during the whole period of captivity, to allow to prisoners of war who are victims of accidents in connection' with their work the enjoyment of the benefit of the provisions applicable to laborers of the same class according to the legislation of the detaining Power. With regard to prisoners of war to whom these legal provisions might not be applied by reason of the legislation of that Power, the latter undertakes to recommend to its legislative body all proper measures equitably to indemnify the victims.

CHAPTER 2. Organization of the Labor.

ARTICLE 28.

The detaining Power shall assume entire responsibility for the maintenance, care, treatment and payment of wages of prisoners of war working for the account of private persons.

ARTICLE 29.

No prisoner of war may be employed at labors for which he is physically unfit.

ARTICLE 30.

The length of the day's work of prisoners of war, including therein the trip going and returning, shall not be excessive and must not, in any case, exceed that allowed for the civil workers in the region employed at the same work. Every prisoner shall be allowed a rest of twenty-four consecutive hours every week, preferably on Sunday.

CHAPTER 3. Prohibited labor.

ARTICLE 31.

Labor furnished by prisoners of war shall have no direct relation with war operations. It is especially prohibited to use prisoners for manufacturing and transporting arms or munitions of any kind or for transporting material intended for combatant units.

In case of violation of the provisions of the preceding paragraph, prisoners, after executing or beginning to execute the order, shall be free to have their protests presented through the mediation of the agents whose functions are set forth in Articles 43 and 44, or, in the absence of an agent, through the mediation of representatives of the protecting Power.

ARTICLE 32.

It is forbidden to use prisoners of war at unhealthful or dangerous work.

Any aggravation of the conditions of labor by disciplinary measures is forbidden.

CHAPTER 4. Labor Detachments

ARTICLE 33.

The system of labor detachments must be similar to that of prisoners-of-war camps, particularly with regard to sanitary conditions, food, attention in case of accident or sickness, correspondence and the receipt of packages.

Every labor detachment shall be dependent on a prisoners' camp. The commander of this camp shall be responsible for the observation, in the labor detachment, of the provisions of the present Convention.

CHAPTER 5. WAGES.

ARTICLE 34.

Prisoners of war shall not receive wages for work connected with the administration, management and maintenance of the camps.

Prisoners utilized for other work shall be entitled to wages to be fixed by agreements between the belligerents.

These agreements shall also specify the part which the camp administration may retain, the amount which shall belong to the prisoner of war and the manner in that amount shall be put at his disposal during the period of his captivity.

While awaiting the conclusion of the said agreements, payment for labor of prisoners shall be settled according to the rules given below:

a) Work done for the State shall be paid for in accordance with the rates in force for soldiers. of the national army doing the same work, or, if none exists, ac cording to a rate in harmony with the work performed.

b) When the work is done for the account of other public administrations or for private persons, conditions shall be regulated by agreement with the military authority.

The pay remaining to the credit of the prisoner shall be delivered to him at the end of his captivity. In case of death, it shall be forwarded through the diplomatic channel to the heirs of the deceased.

SECTION IV. EXTERNAL RELATIONS OF PRISONERS OF WAR.

ARTICLE 35.

Upon the outbreak of hostilities, belligerents shall publish the measures provided for the execution of the provisions of this section.

ARTICLE 36.

Each of the belligerents shall periodically determine the number of letters and postal cards per month which prisoners of war of the various classes shall be allowed to send, and shall inform the other belligerent of this number. These letters and cards shall be transmitted by post by the shortest route. They may not be delayed or retained for disciplinary reasons.

Within a period of not more than one week after his arrival at the camp, and likewise in case of sickness, every prisoner shall be enabled to write his family a postal card

informing it of his capture and of the state of his health. The said postal cards shall be forwarded as rapidly as possible and may not be delayed in any manner.

As a general rule, correspondence of prisoners shall be written in their native language. Belligerents may allow correspondence in other languages.

ARTICLE 37.

Prisoners of war shall be allowed individually to receive parcels by mail, containing foods and other articles intended to supply them with food or clothing. Packages shall be delivered to the addressees and a receipt given.

ARTICLE 38.

Letters and consignments of money or valuables, as well as parcels by post intended for prisoners of war or dispatched by them, either directly, or by the mediation of the information bureaus provided for in Article 77, shall be exempt from all postal duties in the countries of origin and destination, as well as in the countries they pass through.

Presents and relief in kind for prisoners shall be likewise exempt from all import and other duties, as well as of payments for carriage by the State railways.

Prisoners may, in cases of acknowledged urgency, be allowed to send telegrams, paying the usual charges.

ARTICLE 39.

Prisoners of war shall be allowed to receive shipments of books individually, which may be subject to censorship.

Representatives of the protecting Powers and duly recognized and authorized aid societies may send books and collections of books to the libraries of prisoners' camps. The transmission of these shipments to libraries may not be delayed under the pretext of censorship difficulties.

ARTICLE 40.

Censorship of correspondence must be effected within the shortest possible time. Furthermore, inspection of parcels post must be effected under proper conditions to guarantee the preservation of the products which they may contain and, if possible, in the presence of the addressee or an agent duly recognized by him.

Prohibitions of correspondence promulgated by the belligerents for military or political reasons, must be transient in character and as short as possible.

ARTICLE 41.

Belligerents shall assure all facilities for the transmission of instruments, papers or documents intended for prisoners of war or signed by them, particularly of powers of attorney and wills.

They shall take the necessary measures to assure, in case of necessity, the authentication of signatures made by prisoners.

SECTION V. PRISONERS' RELATIONS WITH THE AUTHORITIES.

CHAPTER 1. Complaints of Prisoners of War because of the Conditions of Captivity.

ARTICLE 42.

Prisoners of war shall have the right to inform the military authorities in whose power they are of their requests with regard to the conditions of captivity to which they are subjected.

They shall also have the right to address themselves to representatives of the protecting Powers to indicate to them the points on which they have complaints to formulate with regard to the conditions of captivity.

These requests and complaints must be transmitted immediately.

Even if they am recognized to be unfounded, they may not occasion any punishment.

CHAPTER 2. Representatives of Prisoners of War.

ARTICLE 43.

In every place where there are prisoners of war, they shall be a allowed to appoint agents entrusted with representing them directly with military authorities and protecting Powers.

This appointment shall be subject to the approval of the military authority.

The agents shall be entrusted with the reception and distribution of collective shipments. Likewise, in case the prisoners should decide to organize a mutual assistance system among themselves, this organization would be in the sphere of the agents. Further, they may lend their offices to prisoners to facilitate their relations with the aid societies mentioned in Article 78.

In camps of officers and persons of equivalent status, the senior officer prisoner of the highest rank shall be recognized as intermediary between the camp authorities and the officers and persons of equivalent status who are prisoners. For this purpose, he shall have the power to appoint a prisoner officer to assist him as an interpreter during the conferences with the camp authorities.

ARTICLE 44.

When the agents are employed as laborers, their activity as representatives of prisoners of war must be counted m the compulsory period of labor.

All facilities shall be accorded the agents for their intercourse with the military authorities and with the protecting Power. This intercourse shall not be limited.

No representative of the prisoners may be transferred without the necessary time being allowed him to inform his successors about affairs under consideration.

CHAPTER 3. Penalties Applicable to Prisoners of War.

1. GENERAL PROVISIONS.

ARTICLE 45.

Prisoners of war shall be subject to the laws, regulations, and orders in force in the armies of the detaining Power.
An act of insubordination shall justify the adoption towards them of the measures provided by such laws, regulations and orders.

The provisions of the present chapter, however, are reserved.

ARTICLE 46.

Punishments other than those provided for the same acts for soldiers of the national armies may not be imposed upon prisoners of war by the military authorities and courts of the detaining Power.

Rank being identical, officers, noncommissioned officers or soldiers who are prisoners of war undergoing a disciplinary punishment, shall not be subject to less favorable treatment than that provided in the armies of the detaining Power with regard to the same punishment.

Any corporal punishment, any imprisonment in quarters without daylight and, in general, any form of cruelty, is forbidden.

Collective punishment for individual acts is also forbidden.

ARTICLE 47.

Acts constituting an offense against discipline, and particularly attempted escape, shall be verified immediately; for all prisoners of war, commissioned or not, preventive arrest shall be reduced to the absolute minimum.

Judicial proceedings against prisoners of war shall be conducted as rapidly as the circumstances permit; preventive imprisonment shall be limited as much as possible.

In all cases, the duration of preventive imprisonment shall be deducted from the disciplinary or judicial punishment inflicted, provided that this deduction is allowed for national soldiers.

ARTICLE 48.

Prisoners of war may not be treated differently from other prisoners after having suffered the judicial or disciplinary punishment which has been imposed on them.

However, prisoners punished as a result of attempted escape may be subjected to special surveillance, which, however, may not entail the suppression of the guarantees granted prisoners by the present Convention.

ARTICLE 49.

No prisoner of war may be deprived of his rank by the detaining Power.

Prisoners given disciplinary punishment may not be deprived of the prerogatives attached to their rank. In particular, officers and persons of equivalent status who suffer punishment involving deprivation of liberty shall not be placed in the same quarters as noncommissioned officers or privates being punished.

ARTICLE 50.

Escaped prisoners of war who are retaken before being able to rejoin their own army or to leave the territory occupied by the army which captured them shall be liable only to disciplinary punishment.

Prisoners who, after having succeeded in rejoining their army or in leaving the territory occupied by the army which captured them, may again be taken prisoners, shall not be liable to any punishment on account of their previous flight.

ARTICLE 51.

Attempted escape, even if it is a repetition of the offense, shall not be considered as an aggravating circumstance in case the prisoner of war should be given over to the courts on account of crimes or offenses against persons or property committed in the course of that attempt.

After an attempted or accomplished escape, the comrades of the person escaping who assisted in the escape, may incur only disciplinary punishment on this account.

ARTICLE 52.

Belligerents shall see that the competent authorities exercise the greatest leniency in deciding the question of whether an infraction committed by a prisoner of war should be punished by disciplinary or judicial measures.

This shall be the case especially when it is a question of deciding on acts in connection with escape or attempted escape.

A prisoner may not be punished more than once because of the same act or the same count.

ARTICLE 53.

No prisoner of war on whom a disciplinary punishment has been imposed, who might be eligible for repatriation, maybe kept back because he has not undergone the punishment.

Prisoners to be repatriated who might be threatened with a penal prosecution may be excluded from repatriation until the end of the proceedings and, if necessary, until the completion of the punishment; those who might already be imprisoned by reason of a sentence may be detained until the end of their imprisonment.

Belligerents shall communicate to each other the lists of those who may not be repatriated for the reasons given in the preceding paragraph.

2. DISCIPLINARY PUNISHMENTS.

ARTICLE 54.

Arrest is the most severe disciplinary punishment which may be imposed on a prisoner of war.

The duration of a single punishment may not exceed thirty days.

This maximum of thirty days may not, further, be exceeded in the case of several acts for which the prisoner has to undergo discipline at the time when it is ordered for him, whether or not these acts are connected.

When, during or after the end of a period of arrest, a prisoner shall have a new disciplinary punishment imposed upon him, a space of at least three days shall separate each of the periods of arrest, if one of them is ten days or more.

ARTICLE 55.

Subject to the provisions given in the last paragraph of Article 11, food restrictions allowed in the armies of the detaining Power are applicable, as an increase in punishment, to prisoners of war given disciplinary punishment.

However, these restrictions may be ordered only if the state of health of the prisoners punished permits it.

ARTICLE 56.

In no case may prisoners of war be transferred to penitentiary establishments (prisons, penitentiaries, convict prisons, etc.) there to undergo disciplinary punishment.

The quarters in which they undergo disciplinary punishment shall conform to sanitary requirements.

Prisoners punished shall be enabled to keep themselves in a state of cleanliness.

These prisoners shall every day be allowed to exercise or to stay in the open air at least two hours.

ARTICLE 57.

Prisoners of war given disciplinary punishment shall be allowed to read and write, as well as to send and receive letters.

On the other hand, packages and money sent may be not delivered to the addressees until the expiration of the punishment. If the packages not distributed contain perishable products, these shall be turned over to the camp infirmary or kitchen.

ARTICLE 58.

Prisoners of war given disciplinary punishment shall be allowed, on their request, to be present at the daily medical inspection. They shall receive the care considered

necessary by the doctors and, if necessary, shall be removed to the camp infirmary or to hospitals.

ARTICLE 59.

Excepting the competence of courts and higher military authorities, disciplinary punishment may be ordered only by an officer provided with disciplinary powers in his capacity as commander of a camp or detachment, or by the responsible officer replacing him.

3. JUDICIAL SUITS.

ARTICLE 60.

At the opening of a judicial proceeding directed against a prisoner of war, the detaining Power shall advise the representative of the protecting Power thereof as soon as possible, and always before the date set for the opening of the trial.

This advice shall contain the following information:

a) Civil state and rank of prisoner;

b) Place of sojourn or imprisonment;

c) Specification of the [count] or counts of the indictment, giving the legal provisions applicable.

If it is not possible to mention in that advice the court which will pass upon the matter, the date of opening the trial and the place where it will take place this information must be furnished to the representative of the protecting Power later, as soon as possible, and at all events, at least three weeks before the opening of the trial.

ARTICLE 61.

No prisoner of war may be sentenced without having had an opportunity to defend himself.

No prisoner may be obliged to admit himself guilty of the act of which he is accused.

ARTICLE 62.

The prisoner of war shall be entitled to assistance by a qualified counsel of his choice, and, if necessary, to have recourse to the services of a competent interpreter. He shall be advised of his right by the detaining Power, in due time before the trial.

In default of a choice by the prisoner, the protecting Power may obtain a counsel for him. The detaining Power shall deliver to the protecting Power, on its request, a list of persons qualified to present the defense.
Representatives of the protecting Power shall be entitled to attend the trial of the case.

The only exception to this rule is the case where the trial of the case must be secret in the interest of the safety of the State. The detaining Power should so advise the protecting Power.

ARTICLE 63.

Sentence may be pronounced against a prisoner of war only by the same courts and according to the same procedure as in the case of persons belonging to the armed forces of the detaining Power.

ARTICLE 64.

Every prisoner of war shall have the right of appeal against any sentence rendered with regard to him, in the same way as individuals belonging to the armed forces of the detaining Power.

ARTICLE 65.

Sentences pronounced against prisoners of war shall be communicated to the protecting Power immediately.

ARTICLE 66.

If the death penalty is pronounced against a prisoner of war, a communication setting forth in detail the nature and circumstances of the offense shall be sent as soon as possible to the representative of the protecting Power, for transmission to the Power in whose armies the prisoner served.

The sentence shall not be executed before the expiration of a period of at least three months after this communication.

ARTICLE 67.

No prisoner of war may be deprived of the benefit of the provisions of Article 42 of the present Convention as a result of a sentence or otherwise.

TITLE IV. TERMINATION OF CAPTIVITY.

SECTION 1. DIRECT REPATRIATION AND HOSPITALIZATION IN A NEUTRAL COUNTRY.

ARTICLE 68.

Belligerents are bound to send, back to their own country, regardless of rank or number, seriously sick and seriously injured prisoners of war, after having brought them to a condition where they can be transported.

Agreements between belligerents shall accordingly settle as soon as possible the cases of invalidity or of sickness, entailing direct repatriation, as well as the cases entailing possible hospitalization in a neutral country. While awaiting the conclusion of these agreements, belligerents may have reference to the model agreement annexed, for documentary purposes, to the present Convention.

ARTICLE 69.

Upon the outbreak of hostilities, belligerents shall come to an agreement to name mixed medical commissions. These commissions shall be composed of three members, two of them belonging to a neutral country and one appointed by the detaining Power; one of the physicians of the neutral country shall preside. These mixed medical commissions shall proceed to the examination of sick or wounded prisoners and shall make all due decisions regarding them.

Decisions of these commissions shall he by majority and carried out with the least possible delay.

ARTICLE 70.

Besides those who are designated by the camp physician, the following prisoners of war shall be inspected by the mixed medical Commission mentioned in Article 69, with a view to their direct repatriation or their hospitalization in a neutral country:

a) Prisoners who make such a request directly of the camp physician;

b) Prisoners who are presented by the agents provided for in Article 43, acting on their own initiative or at the request of the prisoners themselves;

c) Prisoners who have been proposed by the Power in whose armies they have served or by an aid society duly recognized and authorized by that Power.

ARTICLE 71.

Prisoners of war who are victims of accidents in connection with work, except

those voluntarily injured, shall enjoy. the benefit of the same provisions, as far as repatriation or possible hospitalization in a neutral country are concerned.

ARTICLE 72.

Throughout the duration of hostilities and for humane considerations, belligerents may conclude agreements with a view to the direct repatriation or hospitalization in a neutral country of able-bodied prisoners of war who have undergone a long period of captivity.

ARTICLE 73.

The expenses of repatriation or of transportation to a neutral country of prisoners of war shall be borne, from the frontiers of the detaining Power, by the Power in whose armies the prisoners. have served.

ARTICLE 74.

No repatriated person may be utilized in active military service.

SECTION II. RELEASE AND REPATRIATION UPON CESSATION OF HOSTILITIES.

ARTICLE 75.

When belligerents conclude a convention of armistice, they must, in principle, have appear therein stipulations regarding the repatriation of prisoners of war. If it has not been possible to insert stipulations in this regard in such convention, belligerents shall nevertheless come to an agreement in this regard as soon as possible. In any case. repatriation of prisoners shall be effected with the least possible delay after the conclusion of peace.

Prisoners of war against whom a penal prosecution might be pending for a crime or an offense of municipal law may, however, be detained until the end of the proceedings and, if necessary, until the expiration of the punishment. The same shall be true of those sentenced for a crime or offense of municipal law.

On agreement between the belligerents, commissions may be established for the purpose of searching for dispersed prisoners and assuring their repatriation.

TITLE V. DEATH OF PRISONERS OF WAR.

ARTICLE 76.

Wills of prisoners of war shall be received and drawn up in the same way as for soldiers of the national army.

The same rules shall be observed regarding death certificates.

Belligerents shall see that prisoners of war dying in captivity are honorably buried and that the graves bear all due information, are respected and properly maintained.

TITLE VI. BUREAUS OF RELIEF AND INFORMATION CONCERNING PRISONERS OF WAR.

ARTICLE 77.

Upon the outbreak of hostilities, each of the belligerent Powers, as well as the neutral Powers which have received belligerents, shall institute an official information bureau for prisoners of war who are within their territory.

Within the shortest possible period, each of the belligerent Powers shall inform its information bureau of every capture of prisoners effected by its armies, giving it all the information regarding identity which it has, allowing it quickly to advise the families concerned, and informing it of the official addresses to which families may write to prisoners.

The information bureau shall immediately forward all this information to the interested Powers, through the intervention, on one hand, of the protecting Powers and, on the other, of the central agency provided for in Article 79.

The information bureau, being charged with replying to all inquiries about of war, shall receive from the various services concerned full information respecting interments, and transfers, releases on parole, repatriations, escapes, stays in hospitals, deaths, as well as other information necessary to enable it to make out and keep up to date an individual return for each prisoner of war.

The bureau shall state in this return, in so far as is possible and subject to the provisions of Article 5: the regimental number, given names and surname, date and place of birth, rank and unit of the interested party, the given name of the father and the name of the mother, the address of the person to be advised in case of accident, wounds, date and place of capture, internment, wounding, and death, as well as any other important information.

Weekly lists containing all new information likely to facilitate the identification of each prisoner shall be transmitted to the interested Powers.

At the conclusion of peace the individual return of the prisoner of war shall be delivered to the Power which he served.

The information bureau shall further be bound to receive all objects of personal use, valuables, letters, pay vouchers, identification marks, etc., which are left by

prisoners of war who have been repatriated, released on parole, escaped or died, and to transmit them to the countries interested.

ARTICLE 78.

Relief societies for prisoners of war, which are properly constituted in accordance with the laws of their country and with the object of serving as the channel for charitable effort, shall receive from the belligerents, for themselves and their duly accredited agents, every facility for the efficient performance of their humane task within the bounds imposed by military necessities. Agents of these societies may be admitted to the camps for the purpose of distributing relief, as also to the halting places of repatriated prisoners, if furnished with a personal permit by the military authorities, and on giving an undertaking in writing to comply with all measures of order and police which the latter may issue.

ARTICLE 79.

A central information agency for prisoners of war shall be created in a neutral country. The International Committee of the Red Cross shall propose the organization of such an agency to the interested Powers, if it considers it necessary.

The function of that agency shall be to centralize all information respecting prisoners, which it may obtain through official or private channels; it shall transmit

it as quickly as possible to the country of origin of the prisoners or to the Power which they have served.

These provisions must not be interpreted as restricting the humanitarian activity of the International Committee of the Red Cross.

ARTICLE 80.

Information bureaus shall enjoy the privilege of free postage on postal matter, as well as all exemptions provided in Article 38.

TITLE VII. APPLICATION OF THE CONVENTION TO CERTAIN CLASSES OF CIVILIANS.

ARTICLE 81.

Individuals who follow armed forces without directly belonging thereto, such as newspaper correspondents and reporters, sutlers, contractors, who fall into the enemy's hands and whom the latter think expedient to detain, shall be entitled to be treated as prisoners of war, provided they are in possession of a certificate from the military authorities of the armed forces which they were accompanying.

TITLE VIII. EXECUTION OF THE CONVENTION.

SECTION I. GENERAL PROVISIONS.

ARTICLE 82.

The provisions of the present Convention must be respected by the High Contracting Parties under all circumstances.

In case, in time of war, one of the belligerents is not a party to the Convention, its provisions shall nevertheless remain in force as between the belligerents who are parties thereto.

ARTICLE 83.

The High Contracting Parties reserve the right to conclude special conventions on all questions relative to prisoners of war, on which it seems to them expedient to have particular regulations.

Prisoners of war shall receive the benefit of these agreements until the completion of repatriation, except in the case of express stipulations to the contrary contained in the above-mentioned agreements or in later agreements, or also except in the case

of more favorable measures taken by one or the other of the belligerent Powers respecting the prisoners which they hold.

In order to assure the reciprocal application of the stipulations of the present Convention, and to facilitate the conclusion of the special conventions provided for above, belligerents may, upon the commencement of hostilities, authorize meetings of representatives of the respective authorities charged with the administration of prisoners of war.

ARTICLE 84.

The text of the present Convention and of the special conventions provided for in the foregoing article, shall be posted, wherever possible in the native language of the prisoners of war, in places where it may be consulted by all the prisoners.

The text of these conventions shall be communicated to prisoners who find it impossible to get the information from the posted text, upon their request.

ARTICLE 85.

The High Contracting Parties shall communicate to one another through the Swiss Federal Council, the official translations of the present Convention as well as of

the laws and regulations which they may come to adopt to assure the application of the present Convention.

SECTION II. ORGANIZATION OF CONTROL.

ARTICLE 86.

The High Contracting Parties recognize that the regular application of the present Convention will find a guaranty in the possibility of collaboration of the protecting Powers charged with safeguarding the interests of belligerents; in this respect, the protecting Powers may, besides their diplomatic personnel, appoint delegates from among their own nationals or from among the nationals of other neutral Powers. These delegates must be subject to the approval of the belligerent near which they exercise their mission.

Representatives of the protecting Power or its accepted delegates shall be permitted to go to any place, without exception, where prisoners of war are interned. They shall have access to all places occupied by prisoners and may interview them, as a general rule without witnesses, personally or through interpreters.

Belligerents shall so far as possible facilitate the task of representatives or accepted delegates of the protecting Power. The military authorities shall be informed of their visit.

Belligerents may come to an agreement to allow persons of the same nationality as the prisoners to be permitted to take part in inspection trips.

ARTICLE 87.

In case of disagreement between the belligerents as to the application of the provisions of the present Convention, the protecting Powers must, in so far as possible, lend their good offices for the purpose of settling the difference. For this purpose, each of the protecting Powers may, in particular, suggest to the interested belligerents a meeting of representatives thereof, possibly upon a neutral territory suitably chosen. Belligerents shall be bound to accede U proposals in this sense which are made to them. The protecting Power may, if occasion arises, submit for the approval of the Powers concerned a person belonging to a neutral Power or a person delegated by the International Committee of the Red Cross, who shall be summoned to take part in this meeting.

ARTICLE 88.

The foregoing provisions are not an obstacle to the humanitarian activity which the International Committee of the Red Cross may use for the protection of prisoners of war, with the consent of the interested belligerents.
SECTION III. FINAL PROVISIONS.

ARTICLE 89.

In the relations between Powers bound by the Hague Convention respecting the Laws and Customs of War on Land, whether it is a question of that of July 29, 1899, or that of October 18, 1907, and who participate in the present Convention, this latter shall complete Chapter 11 of the Regulations annexed to the said Hague Conventions.

ARTICLE 90.

The present Convention, which will bear this day's date, may be signed up to February 1, 1930, on behalf of all the countries represented at the Conference which opened at Geneva July 1, 1929.

ARTICLE 91.

The present Convention shall be ratified as soon as possible.

The ratifications shall be deposited at Berne.

A record of the deposit of each instrument of ratification shall be prepared, a duly certified copy of which shall be forwarded by the Swiss Federal Council to the Governments of all the countries on whose behalf the Convention has been signed or notification of adherence made.

ARTICLE 92.

The present Convention shall become effective six months after the deposit of at least two instruments of ratification.

Subsequently, it shall become effective for each High Contracting Party six months after the deposit of its instrument of ratification.

ARTICLE 93.

From the date on which it becomes effective, the present Convention shall be open for adherences given on behalf of any country in whose name this Convention was not signed.

ARTICLE 94.

Adherence shall be given by written notification addressed to the Swiss Federal Council and shall take effect six months after the date of their receipt.
The Swiss Federal Council shall communicate adherences to the Government of all the countries on whose behalf the Convention was signed or notification of adherence made.

ARTICLE 95.

A state of war shall give immediate effect to ratifications deposited and to adherences; notified by belligerent Powers prior to or after the outbreak of hostilities. The communication of ratifications or adherences received from Powers at war shall be made by the Swiss Federal Council by the most rapid method.

ARTICLE 96.

Each of the High Contracting Parties shall have the right to denounce the present Convention. The denunciation shall not take effect until one year after notification has been made in writing to the Swiss Federal Council. The latter shall communicate such notification to the Governments of all the High Contracting Parties.

The denunciation shall have effect only with respect to the High Contracting Party which gave notification thereof.
Moreover, such denunciation shall not take effect during a war in which the denouncing Power is involved. In this case, the present Convention shall continue, in effect, beyond the period of one year, until the conclusion of peace, and, in any event, until the processes of repatriation axe completed.

ARTICLE 97.

A duly certified copy of the present Convention shall be deposited in the archives of the League of Nations by the Swiss Federal Council. Likewise, ratifications, adherences, and denunciations of which the Swiss Federal Council shall be notified, shall be communicated by it to the League of Nations.

IN FAITH WHEREOF, the Plenipotentiaries named above have signed the present Convention.

DONE at Geneva, the twenty-seventh of July, one thousand nine hundred and twenty-nine, in a single copy, which shall remain in the archives of the Swiss Confederation and duly certified copies of which shall be forwarded to the Governments of all the countries invited to the Conference.

ENDNOTES

Introduction

1   Prisoner figures from *Historical Monograph: Prisoner of War Operations Division, Office of the Provost Marshal General: With Appendices and Supplement, 1945-1946*, 2-3.

2   Judith M. Gansberg, *Stalag U.S.A.: The Remarkable Story of German POWs in America* (New York: Thomas Y. Crowell Co., 1977); Arnold Krammer, *Nazi Prisoners of War in America* (New York: Stein and Day, 1979); Richard P. Walker, *Lone Star and the Swastika: Prisoners of War in Texas* (Austin: Eakin Press, 2001); Michael Waters, *Lone Star Stalag: German Prisoners of War at Camp Hearne* (College Station: Texas A&M University Press, 2004); Lewis H. Carlson, *We Were Each Other's Prisoners: An Oral History of World War II American and German Prisoners of War* (New York: Basic Books, 1997); Ron Robin, *The Barbed-Wire College: Reeducating German POWs in the United States During World War II* (Princeton: Princeton University Press, 1995); Ronald H. Bailey, "Lessons in Democracy: The Secret and Controversial Attempt to Teach German POWs About Freedom While They Were Still in Captivity," *World War II* (August/September 2009): 52-55; Ulrich Straus, *The Anguish of Surrender: Japanese POWs of World War II* (Seattle: University of Washington Press, 2003).

3   Rudolf Thill, *Adrift in Stormy Times* (Decorah, Iowa: South Bear Press, 2004); Moriji Yamaga, ed., *American Democracy and Its Ways* (Tokyo: Iwanami Shoten, 1947).

Chapter I

1   "Armistice Day," *Huntsville Item*, November 9, 1939, 6.

2   "House Approves Temporary Ban on Sale of Arms," *Washington Post*, August 24, 1935, 1. Nat Patton's voting record on the 1937 revision to the 1935 Neutrality Act is available online: "To Agree to S.J. RES 3 (PUB. RES. 1), A Resolution to Regulate Commerce in Firearms, Making Illegal the Exportation of Weapons to Spain," Jan 06, 1937 (75th Congress), https://www.govtrack.us/congress/votes/75-1/h2; "To Pass S.J. RES. 51

(P. RES. 27), The Neutrality Act of 1937," March 18, 1937 (75th Congress), https://www.govtrack.us/congress/votes/75-1/h19; "Congressman Nat Patton Explains the Neutrality Act to Service Clubs Here," *Huntsville Item*, September 7, 1939, 1; "Texas Congressmen Nearly 100 Per Cent in Favor of Lifting Embargo, Cash and Carry Policy Urged in Amendment," *Dallas Morning News*, September 14, 1939, 5; "Congressman Patton Favors Cash and Carry Plan Selling," *Alto Herald* (Alto, Texas), September 21, 1939, 1.

3   "An Invitation to Mr. Adolph (sic) Hitler," *Huntsville Item*, October 19, 1939, 3.

4   Hubert M. Harrison, "Duties of Democracy," *Huntsville Item*, October 3, 1940, 6. On local aid to Finland, see *"Huntsville Item* to Participate in National Drive to Aid Finns," *Huntsville Item*, January 4, 1940, 1.

5   John T. Baldwin to John W. Thomason, Jr., February 11, 1941, Huntsville Prisoner of War Camp Files, Thomason Special Collections Room, Newton Gresham Library, Sam Houston State University.

6   "The New Army," *Huntsville Item*, August 7, 1941, 6.

7   "Memorandum on Engineering Features of 7,000-Man Cantonment near Riverside, Texas," January 1, 1942, Record Group 389 (RG 389), Provost Marshal General's Office (PMGO), Prisoner of War Operations Division, Operations Branch, Subject Correspondence File, 1942-1946, Box 1423, Huntsville, Texas, Construction, Modern Military Records Branch, National Archives, College Park, Maryland (MMRB).

8   The January 18, 1942 report is discussed in Allen W. Gullion, Provost Marshal General, "Memorandum for the Chief of Staff," March 3, 1942, RG 389, PMGO, Prisoner of War Operations Division, Operations Branch, Subject Correspondence File, 1942-1946, Box 1423, Huntsville, Texas, Construction, MMRB. For the February 20 report of the Army Corp of Engineers, see "Memorandum on Engineering Features of Site for Alien Enemy Internment Camp near Huntsville, Texas," February 26, 1942, RG 389, PMGO, Prisoner of War Operations Division, Operations Branch, Subject Correspondence File, 1942-1946, Box 1423, Huntsville, Texas, Construction, MMRB. For the February 24, 1942 approval of the camp site, see: George E. Monk, Major, Quarter Master Corps, Executive Officers, Aliens Division to Chief of Engineers, February 24, 1942, RG 389, PMGO, Prisoner of War Operations Division, Operations Branch, Subject Correspondence File, 1942-1946, Box 1423, Huntsville, Texas, Construction, MMRB. For the March 18, 1942 approval, see: Richard P. Walker, *Lone Star and the Swastika: Prisoners of War in Texas* (Austin: Eakin Press, 2001), 4.

9   Frances Handley Bowers, "History of the Country Campus," (Master's Thesis, Sam Houston State Teachers College, 1950), 7. Bowers spelled

Szilagyi's name, Zilagi, and incorrectly identified him as a member of the Army Corps of Engineers. For Szilagyi's biography and a photo of him, see "Donovan Now City's Top Army Figure; General Is Often Brusque but He's Quick to Smile," *Dallas Morning News*, December 3, 1942, 6. Sam Dominey interviewed by Will Anderson, curator of HEARTS Museum, Huntsville, Texas, March 29, 2011; "An Order Authorizing the Tax Assessor-Collector of Walker County, Texas, to Exempt Certain Property in Possession of the United States Government," May 10, 1943, Walker County Clerk's Office; Maggie Dominey to Nat Patton, October 17, 1942, Nat Patton to Major General Allen Gullion, October 21, 1942, Colonel B. M. Bryan to Nat Patton, October 22, 1942, RG 389, PMGO, Prisoner of War Operations Division, Operations Branch, Subject Correspondence File, 1942-1946, Box 1423, Huntsville, Texas, Construction, MMRB.

10   Principal Engineer, War Department, Galveston Texas, "Alien Enemy Internment Camp, Huntsville, Texas," April 18, 1942, RG 389, PMGO, Prisoner of War Operations Division, Operations Branch, Subject Correspondence File, 1942-1946, Box 1423, Huntsville, Texas, Construction, MMRB. B.M. Bryan, Lt. Col, Chief, Aliens Division, "Memo," April 25, 1942, RG 389, PMGO, Prisoner of War Operations Division, Operations Branch, Subject Correspondence File, 1942-1946, Box 1423, Huntsville, Texas, Construction, MMRB. For the May 12 construction date, see Bowers, "History of the Country Campus," 8.

11   Walker, *The Lone Star and the Swastika*, 3.

12   "Memorandum on Engineering Features of Site for Alien Enemy Internment Camp near Huntsville, Texas," February 26, 1942, RG 389, PMGO, Prisoner of War Operations Division, Operations Branch, Subject Correspondence File, 1942-1946, Box 1423, Huntsville, Texas, Construction, MMRB. Arnold P. Krammer, "German Prisoners of War in the United States," *Military Affairs* 40 (April 1976), 68. Japan signed the Geneva Accords of 1929, but failed to ratify the document. Nevertheless, in 1942, Japan indicated that it would follow the Geneva Accords' rules for the treatment of POWs. During the war, however, Japan violated the accords by mistreating, torturing, and killing POWs.

13   Bowers, "History *of the Country Campus," 10-12; Walker,* Lone Star and the Swastika, 6. One of the Fretz company's local secretaries, Mary Andrews, was the sister of actor Dana Andrews, a major Hollywood star of the 1940s.

14   Bowers, "History of the Country Campus," 10-12; Waters, *Lone Star Stalag*, 8; Walker, *Lone Star and the Swastika*, 6.

15   Rudolph Fischer and Charles Eberhardt, "Department of State Special Division Inspection Report, Prisoner of War Camp, Camp Huntsville," December 4 and 5, 1943, RG 389, PMGO, Enemy POW Information

Bureau, Reporting Branch Subject File, 1942-1946, Box 2664, Inspection and Field Reports (Houlton to Jerome), MMRB.

16   "Prisoner of War Camp Bus Stop Named Carvolth," *Huntsville Item*, October 7, 1943, 8.

17   "Soldiers to Garrison the Camp Near Here," *Huntsville Item*, August 27, 1942, 1; "Hundreds Visit Camp Open House Friday," *Huntsville Item*, September 24, 1942, 1.

18   "Howdy Soldiers!," *Huntsville Item*, September 24, 1942, 6; "H. M. Stougaard Gives Plants To Beautify Camp," *Huntsville Item*, October 8, 1942, 1.

19   Major A.H. Kemp, "Construction Changes," September 29, 1942, RG 389, PMGO, Prisoner of War Operations Division, Operations Branch, Subject Correspondence File, 1942-1946, Box 1423, Huntsville, Texas, Construction, MMRB; Brigadier General, W.A. Wood, "Construction of Officers' Prisoner of War Camps." January 4, 1943, RG 389, PMGO, Prisoner of War Operations Division, Operations Branch, Subject Correspondence File, 1942-1946, Box 1423, Huntsville, Texas, Construction, MMRB; Brigadier General, B.M. Bryan, Memorandum, February 9, 1943, RG 389, PMGO, Prisoner of War Operations Division, Operations Branch, Subject Correspondence File, 1942-1946, Box 1423, Huntsville, Texas, Construction, MMRB.

20   Krammer, *Nazi Prisoners of War in America*, 2-3; Richard Evans, *The Coming of the Third Reich* (New York: Penguin Press, 2003), 340.

21   Krammer, *Nazi Prisoners of War in America*, 3-13.

22   Brigadier General, W.A. Wood to Chief of Engineers, U.S. Army, December 28, 1942, RG 389, PMGO, Prisoner of War Operations Division, Operations Branch, Subject Correspondence File, 1942-1946, Box 1423, Huntsville, Texas, Construction, MMRB; Brigadier General, W.A. Wood to Chief of Engineers, U.S. Army, January 4, 1943, RG 389, PMGO, Prisoner of War Operations Division, Operations Branch, Subject Correspondence File, 1942-1946, Box 1423, Huntsville, Texas, Construction, MMRB; Lt. Col. W.G. Saville to PMGO, January 19, 1943, RG 389, PMGO, Prisoner of War Operations Division, Operations Branch, Subject Correspondence File, 1942-1946, Box 1423, Huntsville, Texas, Construction, MMRB; Lt. Col. Charles Keller Jr. to Chief of Engineers, U.S. Army, February 23, 1943, RG 389, PMGO, Prisoner of War Operations Division, Operations Branch, Subject Correspondence File, 1942-1946, Box 1423, Huntsville, Texas, Construction, MMRB; Brigadier General, B.M. Bryan, Memorandum, March 2, 1943, RG 389, PMGO, Prisoner of War Operations Division, Operations Branch, Subject Correspondence File, 1942-1946, Box 1423, Huntsville, Texas, Construction, MMRB.

23   "Lt. Co. H. E. Fischer In Command of Camp," *Huntsville Item*, August 20, 1942, 1. "Lt. Col. Fischer Is Rotary Club Speaker Tuesday," *Huntsville Item*, January 28, 1943, 5; "Famed Afrika Korps Chops Trees in Texas, " *Huntsville Item*, June 3, 1943, 1; Richard S. Warner, "Barbed Wire and Nazilagers: PW Camps in Oklahoma," *The Chronicles of Oklahoma* 64 (Spring 1986): 36-67.

24   "Galveston Girl First Sgt Major", *San Antonio Light*, October 28, 1942; "He Wears A Pair of Khaki Pants," *The Huntsville Item*, October 29, 1942.

25   S.W. Lawless to Wilbert Lee O'Daniel, March 11, 1943, RG 389, PMGO, Prisoner of War Operations Division, Operations Branch, Subject Correspondence File, 1942-1946, Box 1429, (Misc. Douglas, Wyo. To Ft. Meade, Maryland), MMRB.

26   Allen Ludden's columns under the titles "He Wears a Pair of Khaki Pants" and "See Here Private" appeared in the *Huntsville Item* on October 8, 15, 22, 29, November 4, 12, 26, and December 3. Gordon T. Miller's columns under the titles "See Here Private" and "News from the Camp" appeared in the *Huntsville Item* on December 24 and 31, January 7, 14, 21, 28, February 4, 14, 18, 25, March 4, 11, 18, 25, and April 1 and 8. On the arrival of Colonel Joseph R. Carvolth see, "Colonel Carvolth is Assigned to the Huntsville Camp," *Huntsville Item*, April 29, 1943, 1.

27   In addition to the columns by the camp personnel cited above, see: "Officers Club At Camp Is Opened With Dance," *Huntsville Item*, October 8, 1942, 4; "Prison Orchestra to Play at Camp Dance," *Huntsville Item*, February 4, 1943, 1.

28   "Soldiers At Camp Entertained By Broadcast Group," *Huntsville Item*, January 21, 1943, 8; "Huntsville Camp Library and Chapel Are Opened," *Huntsville Item*, February 25, 1943, 1.

29   R.A. Anderson interviewed by Norma Brown, November 1, 2001, Walker County Stories, Thomason Special Collections Room, Newton Gresham Library, Sam Houston State University.

Chapter II

1   For date first POW received at Camp Huntsville, see: D.L. Schwieger, Captain, Field Liaison Officer and E.C. Shannahan, Major, Field Liaison Officer, Memorandum for Colonel Clifford S. Urwiller, Chief Labor and Liaison Branch, February 12, 1945, RG 389, PMGO, Enemy POW Information Bureau, Reporting Branch Subject File, 1942-1946, Box 2664, Inspection and Field Reports (Houlton to Jerome), MMRB.

2   Vernon Fitzgerald Schuder interviewed by Frances Handley Bowers as noted in *History of Country Campus*, 13; Donna Coffen interviewed by authors, March 5, 2011; R.A. Anderson interviewed by Norma Brown, November 1, 2001, Walker County Stories, Thomason Special Collections Room, Newton Gresham Library, Sam Houston State University; Walker, *Lone Star and the Swastika*, 51; Steve Brewer, "Memories of WWII camp alive after 40 years," *Huntsville Item*, April 16, 1989, 1C.

3   Nina Mickelwait Collier interviewed by SHSU student, April 6, 2000, in Jeffrey L. Littlejohn's possession.

4   Antonio Thompson, *Men in German Uniform* (Knoxville: University of Tennessee Press, 2010), 38, 50-52.

5   Ibid.

6   Sigman Byrd, "Hans is a Mighty Lucky Nazi," *Houston Post, Sunday Magazine*, June 20, 1943, 5.

7   Oberschütze Siebenbrot interviewed by Martin Schenkel, January 23, 1999, for "Interview with an Afrikakorps Infantry Veteran," http://www.feldgrau.com/interview2.html.

8   Robert Ebinger to Erna Meckler, August 11, 1943 and April 28, 1944 in Jeffery L. Littlejohn's possession.

9   Franz Büczolich to Anni Buczolich, January 3, 1944, in Jeffrey L. Littlejohn's possession.

10   Jennifer Lightsey, "Changing Bad Memories to Good Memories," *Huntsville Item*, August 10, 1994, 1.

11   Robert Ebinger to Erna Meckler, April 28, 1944 in Jeffery L. Littlejohn's possession.

12   Ingeborg Osterhout interviewed by Carolyn Carroll, June 14, 2012. Osterhout's father, Johnann Klassek, was a prisoner at Camp Huntsville. His experience is covered in Hermann Jung, *Die deutschen Kriegsgefangenen in amerikanischer Hand, USA* (Munich, Germany: Verlang Ernst und Werner Gieseking, Bielefeld, 1972), 38,83, 188.

13   Arnold P. Krammer, "When the 'Afrika Korps' Came to Texas," *The Southwestern Historical Quarterly* Vol. 80 No. 3 (Jan., 1977), 264-269.

14   "German Prisoners of War: They March, Play and Work at a Huntsville, Texas, Camp," *New York Times*, June 15, 1943, 3.

15   Thill, *Adrift in Stormy Times*, 154; Byrd, "Hans is a Mighty Lucky Nazi," *Houston Post, Sunday Magazine*, June 20, 1943, 5.

16   Thill, *Adrift in Stormy Times*, 155, 164-165.

17   Titus Fields interviewed by authors, March 5, 2012, in Jeffrey L. Littlejohn's possession; Krammer, "When the 'Afrika Korps' Came to Texas," 264-270; "Nazis Hoe Cotton," *Business Week*, June 19, 1943, 18; Jung, *Die deutschen Kriegsgefangenen in amerikanischer Hand*, USA, 189.

18   "Walker County Farmers To Use War Prisoners," *Huntsville Item*, June 3, 1943, 1; "Item Staff Member Sees War Prisoners Chop Cotton," *Huntsville Item*, June 24, 1943, 1; Jackie Dodge, letter dated February 10, 1997, recounting husband Fred K. Dodge's stories of working with the POWs, copy in Jeffrey L. Littlejohn's possession.

19   Krammer, "When the 'Afrika Korps' Came to Texas," 264-270.

20   W.O. Simmons interviewed by Robert W. Tissing, Jr., May 30, 1972, in "Utilization of World War II Prisoners of War in Texas: Oral Memoirs," Baylor University Archives, http://digitalcollections.baylor.edu/cdm/compoundobject/collection/buioh/id/3015/rec/8

21   Rudolph Fischer and Charles Eberhardt, "Department of State Special Division Inspection Report, Prisoner of War Camp, Camp Huntsville," December 4 and 5, 1943, RG 389, PMGO, Enemy POW Information Bureau, Reporting Branch Subject File, 1942-1946, Box 2664, Inspection and Field Reports (Houlton to Jerome), MMRB.

22   James G. Gee interviewed by Robert W. Tissing, Jr., May 30, 1972, in "Utilization of World War II Prisoners of War in Texas: Oral Memoirs," Baylor University Archives, http://digitalcollections.baylor.edu/cdm/compoundobject/collection/buioh/id/3015/rec/8

23   Titus Fields interviewed by authors, March 5, 2012, in Jeffrey L. Littlejohn's possession.

24   Rudolph Fischer and Charles Eberhardt, "Department of State Special Division Inspection Report, Prisoner of War Camp, Camp Huntsville," December 4 and 5, 1943, RG 389, PMGO, Enemy POW Information Bureau, Reporting Branch Subject File, 1942-1946, Box 2664, Inspection and Field Reports (Houlton to Jerome), MMRB; Walker, *Lone Star and the Swastika*, 37-38.

25   Walker, *Lone Star and the Swastika*, 41-44.

26   Klaūs Labeth to the Family of Emil Labeth, June 16, 1944, in Jeffrey L. Littlejohn's possession.

27   Steve Brewer, "Memories of WWII camp alive after 40 years," *Huntsville Item*, April 16, 1989, 1C.

28   Quoted in Hermann Jung, *Die duetschen Kriegsgefangenen in amerikanischer Hand-USA*, 42-45.

29   Titus Fields interviewed by authors, March 5, 2012, in Jeffrey L. Littlejohn's possession; Arnold P. Krammer "German Prisoners of War in The United States," *Military Affairs* Vol. 40, No. 2 (April 1976): 68-73.

30   Karl-Heinz Blumenthal, "My Return After 60 Years to a POW Camp in Texas," http://home.arcor.de/kriegsgefangene/memoirs/karl_blumenthal.htm; see also, Suzanne Staetter, "POW Held Here Returns: Former German Prisoner Comes Back After 36 Years," *Huntsville Item*, June 1, 1979, 9A.

31   Titus Fields interviewed by authors, March 5, 2012, in Jeffrey L. Littlejohn's possession.

32   Linda Evans, "Former Camp Home to Faculty Family," *Huntsville Item*, October 23, 1996, 8B.

33   Letter from Brig. Gen. B.M. Bryan, Director Alien Division, PMGO to Commanding Generals, All Service Compounds, February 5, 1943, in PMGO, *POW Operations*, OCMH, vol 1-2, append., vol 1 of 3 of Tabs, Tab 6, PMGO, *POW Operations*, OCMH, 1:75; Jung, *Die deutschen Kriegsgefangenen in amerikanischer Hand, USA*, 42-45; POW Circular No. 35, July 1, 1944, in PMGO, *POW Operations*, OCMH vol 1-2, append., Tab 8; Donna Coffen interviewed by authors, March 5, 2011, in Jeffrey L. Littlejohn's possession.

34   Jung, *Die deutschen Kriegsgefangenen in amerikanischer Hand, USA*, 53.

35   Brewer, "Memories of WWII camp alive after 40 years," *Huntsville Item*, April 16, 1989, 1C; Photos from Kathleen Newman Skains, granddaughter of camp electrician, Charlie F. Parker; Blumenthal, "My Return After 60 Years"; Bowers, "History of Country Campus," 13-15; Richard P. Walker, *Lone Star and the Swastika*, 70-71; Schenkel, "Adventures of an Afrikakorps Infantry Veteran."

36   Blumenthal, "My Return After 60 Years"; Schenkel, "The Adventures of an Afrikakorps Infantry Veteran"; Titus Fields interviewed by authors, March 5, 2012, in Jeffrey L. Littlejohn's possession; Arnold Krammer, "When the 'Afrika Korps' Came to Texas," 261-262.

37   Alfred L. Cardinaux report on Camp Huntsville for the International Red Cross, June 7, 1943, RG 389, PMGO, Enemy POW Information Bureau, Reporting Branch Subject File, 1942-1946, Box 2664, Inspection and Field Reports (Houlton to Jerome), MMRB; Rudolph Fischer and Charles Eberhardt, "Department of State Special Division Inspection Report, Prisoner of War Camp, Camp Huntsville," December 4 and 5, 1943, RG 389, PMGO, Enemy POW Information Bureau, Reporting Branch Subject File, 1942-1946, Box 2664, Inspection and Field Reports (Houlton to Jerome), MMRB.Rudolph Fischer and Eldon F. Nelson report on Camp Huntsville, April 12, 1944, RG 389, PMGO, Enemy POW Information Bureau, Reporting Branch Subject File, 1942-1946, Box 2664, Inspection and Field Reports (Houlton to Jerome), MMRB; Paul A. Neuland, "Field Service Report on Visit to Prisoner of War Camp, Huntsville, Texas, on 17-18 January 1945, by Captain Alexander Lakes," February 7, 1945, RG 389, PMGO, POW Special Projects Division, Administrative Branch Decimal File 1943-46, Box 1615, Camp Haan to Camp Huntsville, MMRB.

38   John Warren Smith, "Doing One's Unhappy Duty," *Huntsville Item*, January 21, 2001, 4C.

39   Linda Evans, "Former Camp Home to Faculty Family," *Huntsville Item*, October 23, 1996, 8B.

40   *Historical Monograph: Prisoner of War Operations Division, Office of the Provost Marshal General: With Appendices and Supplement, 1945-1946*, 30.

41   Donna Coffen interviewed by authors, March 5, 2011, in Jeffrey L. Littlejohn's possession.

42   Paul A. Neuland, "Field Service Report on Visit to Prisoner of War Camp, Huntsville, Texas, on 17-18 January 1945, by Captain Alexander Lakes," February 7, 1945, RG 389, PMGO, POW Special Projects Division, Administrative Branch Decimal File 1943-46, Box 1615, Camp Haan to Camp Huntsville, MMRB.

43   "War Prisoner Probe," *Fort Worth Star-Telegram*, February 21, 1945 and "War-Prisoners' Treatment By Germans and Japanese," *San Antonio Express*, February 21, 1945 both in RG389, PMGO, Entry 439A: "Historical File, 1941-1958," Box 37, "Prisoner of War Operations," MMRB.

44   "Geneva Convention Explained at Kiwanis Today," *Huntsville Item*, May 3, 1945, 5; "Dr. McGee Is Speaker at Rotary Club," *Huntsville Item*, May 24, 1945, 12.

45   Wilhelm Sauerbrei quoted in Krammer, "German Prisoners of War in the United States," 72.

46   Tom Pickett to Major General James A. Ulio, May 31, 1945, and Archer Lench to Tom Pickett, June 21 1945, RG 389, PMGO, Prisoner of War Operations Division, Operations Branch, Subject Correspondence File, 1942-1946, Box 1429 (Misc. Douglas, Wyo. To Ft. Meade, Maryland), MMRB.

47   Titus Fields interviewed by authors, March 5, 2012, in Jeffrey L. Littlejohn's possession.

48   Ibid; "Nazi Prisoner Caught," *Dallas Morning News*, February 26, 1944, 4; Rudolph Fischer and Eldon F. Nelson report on Camp Huntsville, April 12, 1944, RG 389, PMGO, Enemy POW Information Bureau, Reporting Branch Subject File, 1942-1946, Box 2664, Inspection and Field Reports (Houlton to Jerome), MMRB; Krammer, "When the 'Afrika Korps' Came to Texas," 264-270.

49   Gansberg, *Stalag U.S.A.*, 44; Fincher, "By Convention, the Enemy within Never Did Without," *Smithsonian* Vol. 26, No. 3 (June 1995), 126.

50   Krammer, "When the 'Afrika Korps' Came to Texas," 264-270; Blackshear M. Bryan, "Statement on Enemy Prisoners of War in the United States, by Brigadier General B.M. Bryan, Jr., Assistant, The Provost Marshal General, Before Military Affairs Committee of the House of Representatives, Thursday, April 25, 1945," File 383.6 Gen P/W Prisoner of War Operations Volume 2 of 3, Historical Manuscript File, War Department Special Staff Historical Division File No 4-4.

Chapter III

1   On the situation with POW guards nationally, see: Gansberg, *Stalag U.S.A.*, 42-44, and Thompson, *Men in German Uniform*, 50-52. For local sources on Huntsville, see: R.A. Anderson interviewed by Norma Brown, November 1, 2001, Walker County Stories, Thomason Special Collections Room, Newton Gresham Library, Sam Houston State University; Titus Fields interviewed by authors, March 5, 2012, in Jeffrey L. Littlejohn's possession.

2   Thompson, *Men in German Uniform*, 87-91; I.B. Summers, "Transfer of German Prisoners of War," July 29, 1943, RG 389, PMGO, Enemy POW Information Bureau, Reporting Branch Subject File, 1942-1946, Box 2480, Camps—Front Royal Remount Depot to Huntsville, MMRB; Joseph R. Carvolth, "Nazi Activities," September 7, 1943, RG 389, PMGO, Enemy POW Information Bureau, Reporting Branch Subject File, 1942-1946, Box 2480, Camps—Front Royal Remount Depot to Huntsville, MMRB.

3   I.B. Summers, "Transfer of German Prisoners of War," July 29, 1943, RG 389, PMGO, Enemy POW Information Bureau, Reporting Branch Subject File, 1942-1946, Box 2480, Camps—Front Royal Remount Depot to Huntsville,

MMRB; Joseph R. Carvolth, "Nazi Activities," September 7, 1943, RG 389, PMGO, Enemy POW Information Bureau, Reporting Branch Subject File, 1942-1946, Box 2480, Camps - Front Royal Remount Depot to Huntsville, MMRB; Thill, *Adrift in Stormy Times*, 151-166.

4   Paul A. Neuland, "Field Service Report on Visit to Prisoner of War Camp, Huntsville, Texas, on 17-18 January 1945, by Captain Alexander Lakes," February 7, 1945, RG 389, PMGO, POW Special Projects Division, Administrative Branch Decimal File 1943-46, Box 1615, Camp Haan to Camp Huntsville, MMRB.

5   Letter, Headquarters, ASF to Commanding General, All Service Commands, March 24, 1944, File 383.6 Gen P/W Prisoner of War Operations Volume II of 3 Volumes, Historical Manuscript File, War Department Special Staff Historical Division File No 4-4, World War II Operational Documents, Combined Arms Research Library, Fort Leavenworth, Kansas. http://cgsc. contentdm.oclc.org/cdm/compoundobject/collection/p4013coll8/id/2131/ rec/2.

6   Waters, *Lone Star Stalag*, 95-110; Walker, *Lone Star and the Swastika*, 88.

7   John Crissy, "Transfer of Prisoners of War to Camp McCain, Mississippi," December 24, 1943, RG 389, PMGO, Enemy POW Information Bureau, Reporting Branch Subject File, 1942-1946, Box 2480, Camps—Front Royal Remount Depot to Huntsville, MMRB; Earl Edwards, "Transfer of German Prisoners of War," January 10, 1944, RG 389, PMGO, Enemy POW Information Bureau, Reporting Branch Subject File, 1942-1946, Box 2480, Camps—Front Royal Remount Depot to Huntsville, MMRB.

8   Walker, *Lone Star and the Swastika*, 103; Thill, *Adrift in Stormy Times*, 152-154. Thill's account of how prisoners became mixed was supported by other sources including: Paul A. Neuland, "Field Service Report on Visit to Prisoner of War Camp, Huntsville, Texas, on 17-18 January 1945, by Captain Alexander Lakes," February 7, 1945, RG 389, PMGP, POW Special Projects Division, Administrative Branch Decimal File 1943-46, Box 1615, Camp Haan to Camp Huntsville, MMRB.

9   Carlson, *We Were Each Other's Prisoners*, 176-177; Krammer, *Nazi Prisoners of War in America*, 153-154; Fischer, "By Convention the Enemy Never Did Without," *Smithsonian*, 126.

10   Carlson, *We Were Each Other's Prisoners*, 155-172.

11   Ibid.

12   John Crissy, "Transfer of Prisoners of War to Camp McCain, Mississippi," December 24, 1943, RG 389, PMGO, Enemy POW Information Bureau,

Reporting Branch Subject File, 1942-1946, Box 2480, Camps - Front Royal Remount Depot to Huntsville, MMRB. While no specific reference to the 999th has been found in records related to Camp Huntsville, Colonel Crissy does identify the anti-Nazis as former political prisoners in his memo. This, with Thill's testimony, along with the known presence of 999th members at the other Texas camps, suggests that some of the men originally assigned to Camp Huntsville may have been members of the 999th.

13   Thill, *Adrift in Stormy Times*, 151-166.

14   John Crissy, "Commanding Officer, POW Camp, Huntsville to Commanding General, 8th Service Command," February 15, 1945, RG 389, PMGO, Operations Branch, POW Operations Division, File: 250.1 General P/W #2, Classified Decimal File, Box 1370, MMRB; Walker, *Lone Star and the Swastika*, 105.

15   Rudolph Fischer and Charles Eberhardt, "Department of State Special Division Inspection Report, Prisoner of War Camp, Camp Huntsville," December 4 and 5, 1943, RG 389, PMGO, Enemy POW Information Bureau, Reporting Branch Subject File, 1942-1946, Box 2664, Inspection and Field Reports (Houlton to Jerome), MMRB.

16   Ibid.

17   "Enemy Prisoners of War Under Sentences of Courts-Martial (Through 31 August 1945)," File 383.6 Gen P/W Prisoner of War Operations, Volume

2 of 3, Historical Manuscript File, War Department Special Staff Historical Division File No 4-4.

18   Rudolph Fischer and Charles Eberhardt, "Department of State Special Division Inspection Report, Prisoner of War Camp, Camp Huntsville," December 4 and 5, 1943, RG 389, PMGO, Enemy POW Information Bureau, Reporting Branch Subject File, 1942-1946, Box 2664, Inspection and Field Reports (Houlton to Jerome), MMRB.

19   Paul A. Neuland, "Field Service Report on Visit to Prisoner of War Camp, Huntsville, Texas, on 17-18 January 1945, by Captain Alexander Lakes," February 7, 1945, RG 389, PMGO, POW Special Projects Division, Administrative Branch Decimal File 1943-46, Box 1615, Camp Haan to Camp Huntsville, MMRB.

20   John Crissy, "Transfer of Prisoners of War to Camp McCain, Mississippi," December 24, 1943, RG 389, PMGO, Enemy POW Information Bureau, Reporting Branch Subject File, 1942-1946, Box 2480, Camps—Front Royal Remount Depot to Huntsville, MMRB; Earl Edwards, "Transfer of German Prisoners of War," January 10, 1944, RG 389, PMGO, Enemy POW Information Bureau, Reporting Branch Subject File, 1942-1946, Box

2480, Camps—Front Royal Remount Depot to Huntsville, MMRB; Rudolph Fischer and Charles Eberhardt, "Department of State Special Division Inspection Report, Prisoner of War Camp, Camp Huntsville," December 4 and 5, 1943, RG 389, PMGO, Enemy POW Information Bureau, Reporting Branch Subject File, 1942-1946, Box 2664, Inspection and Field Reports (Houlton to Jerome), MMRB; "Enemy Prisoners of War Under Sentences of Courts-Martial (Through 31 August 1945)," File 383.6 Gen P/W Prisoner of War Operations, Volume 2 of 3, Historical Manuscript File, War Department Special Staff Historical Division File No 4-4.

21   Rudolph Fischer and Charles Eberhardt, "Department of State Special Division Inspection Report, Prisoner of War Camp, Camp Huntsville," December 4 and 5, 1943, RG 389, PMGO, Enemy POW Information Bureau, Reporting Branch Subject File, 1942-1946, Box 2664, Inspection and Field Reports (Houlton to Jerome), MMRB.

22   Rudolph Fischer and Eldon F. Nelson, Report on Camp Huntsville, April 12, 1944, RG 389, PMGO, Enemy POW Information Bureau, Reporting Branch Subject File, 1942-1946, Box 2664, Inspection and Field Reports (Houlton to Jerome), MMRB.

23   Ibid.

24   Titus Fields interviewed by authors, March 5, 2012, in Jeffrey L. Littlejohn's possession.

25   Letter, Headquarters, ASF to Commanding General, All Service Commands, March 24, 1944, File 383.6 Gen P/W Prisoner of War Operations Volume II of 3 Volumes, Historical Manuscript File, War Department Special Staff Historical Division File No 4-4, World War II Operational Documents, Combined Arms Research Library, Fort Leavenworth, Kansas. http://cgsc.contentdm.oclc.org/cdm/compoundobject/collection/p4013coll8/id/2131/rec/2.

26   Titus Fields interviewed by authors, March 5, 2012, in Jeffrey L. Littlejohn's possession; Thill, *Adrift in Stormy Times*, 153-160; Krammer, *Nazi Prisoners of War in America*, 150; "Afrika Korps Youths Chop Texas Cotton: War Prisoner Camp New Huntsville Enclosed with Wire," *Dallas Morning News*, June 15, 1943, 6.

27   Paul A. Neuland, "Field Service Report on Visit to Prisoner of War Camp, Huntsville, Texas, on 17-18 January 1945, by Captain Alexander Lakes," February 7, 1945, RG 389, PMGO, POW Special Projects Division, Administrative Branch Decimal File 1943-46, Box 1615, Camp Haan to Camp Huntsville, MMRB; Fincher, "By Convention, the Enemy within Never Did Without," 126.

28   D.L. Schwieger and E.C. Shannahan, "Report of visit to Prisoner of War Camp, Huntsville, Texas on 9-10 February 1945," RG 389, PMGO, Enemy POW Information Bureau, Reporting Branch Subject File, 1942-1946, Box 2664, Inspection and Field Reports (Houlton to Jerome), MMRB; Walker, *Lone Star and the Swastika*, 103.

29   Rudolph Fischer and Charles Eberhardt, "Department of State Special Division Inspection Report, Prisoner of War Camp, Camp Huntsville," December 4 and 5, 1943, RG 389, PMGO, Enemy POW Information Bureau, Reporting Branch Subject File, 1942-1946, Box 2664, Inspection and Field Reports (Houlton to Jerome), MMRB; Rudolph Fischer and Eldon F. Nelson report on Camp Huntsville, April 12, 1944, RG 389, PMGO, Enemy POW Information Bureau, Reporting Branch Subject File, 1942-1946, Box 2664, Inspection and Field Reports (Houlton to Jerome), MMRB; Paul A. Neuland, "Field Service Report on Visit to Prisoner of War Camp, Huntsville, Texas, on 17-18 January 1945, by Captain Alexander Lakes," February 7, 1945, RG 389, PMGO, POW Special Projects Division, Administrative Branch Decimal File 1943-46, Box 1615, Camp Haan to Camp Huntsville, MMRB.

Chapter IV

1   Walker, *Lone Star and the Swastika*, 87.

2   Headquarters Army Service Forces, Office of the Adjutant General, Letter, From Headquarters, ASF to Commanding General, All Service Commands, February 6, 1944, File 383.6 Gen P/W Prisoner of War Operations Volume II of 3 Volumes, Historical Manuscript File, War Department Special Staff Historical Division File No 4-4, Command and General Staff College. Headquarters Army Service Forces, Office of the Adjutant General, Memorandum, "German Prisoner of War Spokesmen and Supervisors," March 24, 1944 File 383.6 Gen P/W Prisoner of War Operations Volume I of 3 Volumes, Historical Manuscript File, War Department Special Staff Historical Division File No 4-4, Command and General Staff College; Walker, *Lone Star and the Swastika*, 87.

3   This Technical Manual was really just a collection of letters, circulars, and memoranda many of which are contained in File 383.6 Gen P/W Prisoner of War Operations Volumes 1 to 3, Historical Manuscript File, War Department Special Staff Historical Division File No 4-4, Command and General Staff College.

4   Ronald H. Bailey, "The Secret and Controversial Attempt to Teach German POWs About Freedom While They Were Still In Captivity," *World War II* (August/September, 2008), 52-58.

5   Ron Robins, *The Barbed-Wire College* (Princeton: Princeton University Press, 1995), 237

6   Arnold P. Krammer, "German Prisoners of War in the United States," *Military Affairs*, Vol. 40, No. 2 (April, 1976), 68-73.

7   "Many War Prisoners Found Strong Nazis," *The Christian Science Monitor*, November 15, 1943, 9; "Nazis Termed Treacherous by Chaplain," *Duluth Herald*, November 11, 1943; Walker, *Lone Star and the Swastika*, 103-104; Krammer, *Nazi Prisoners of War in America*, 190, 301. On Hall's later promotion and move from Huntsville, see: "Camp Chaplain Transferred and Is Promoted," *Huntsville Item*, December 9, 1943, 6.

8   William L. Shirer, "Start Reeducation on Prisoners: Shirer Advises It, Points Out Conditions in Camps in United States," *Washington Post*, January 23, 1944, B2.

9   Dorothy Thompson, "On The Record," *Milwaukee Sentinel*, April 26, 1944, 12.

10   Krammer, *Nazi Prisoners of War In America*, 191-192.

11   Ibid., 195.

12   Ibid., 196.

13   Bailey, "The Secret and Controversial Attempt to Teach German POWs About Freedom," 52-58.

14   Robins, *The Barbed-Wire College*, 236-237.

15   Krammer, *Nazi Prisoners of War In America*, 196-98, 201.

16   Ibid.

17   Quoted in Krammer, *Nazi Prisoners of War In America*, 202; Waters, *Lone Star Stalag*, 141.

18   Krammer, *Nazi Prisoners of War In America*, 202-204.

19   Paul A. Neuland, "Field Service Report on Visit to Prisoner of War Camp, Huntsville, Texas, on 17-18 January 1945, by Captain Alexander Lakes," February 7, 1945, RG 389, PMGO, POW Special Projects Division, Administrative Branch Decimal File 1943-46, Box 1615, Camp Haan to Camp Huntsville, MMRB.

20   Lt. Colonel Davison letters to Harmon Lowman, president of Sam Houston State Teachers College, March 20, 1945 and April 5, 1945, and Harmon

Lowman letter to Lt Colonel Davison, April 13, 1945, RG 389, PMGO, POW Special Projects Division, Administrative Branch Decimal File 1943-46, Box 1615, Camp Haan to Camp Huntsville, MMRB; Krammer, "German Prisoners of War in the United States," *Military Affairs*, 68-73; Alfred L. Cardinaux report on Camp Huntsville for the International Red Cross, February 18, 1944, RG 389, PMGO, Enemy POW Information Bureau, Reporting Branch Subject File, 1942-1946, Box 2664, Inspection and Field Reports (Houlton to Jerome), MMRB.

21   Krammer, *Nazi Prisoners of War In America*, 206-08.

22   Ibid.

23   Ibid.

24   Ibid., 199-200.

25   Ibid., 217-218.

26   Gansberg, *Stalag, U.S.A.*, 6.

27   Robins, *The Barbed-Wire College*, 110-111.

28   World War II Operational Documents "Re-Education of Enemy Prisoners of War: Projects II and III," March 1, 1946, Historical Section, Office of the Provost Marshal General, Records Group 465/2-4, Combined Arms Research Library Digital Library, http://cgsc.contentdm.oclc.org/cdm/.

29   John R. Williams, "Rev. Prince Insulted! Famous Baptist Leader Slapped by Tex. Officer," *Pittsburgh Courier*, September 17, 1938, 1; "Justice Frankfurter Stays Execution of Condemned Texan," *Philadelphia Tribune*, October 4, 1941, 2; "Sheriff Small Gets Judgment in Libel Suit," *Huntsville Item*, February 22, 1945, 1; James W. Marquart, Sheldon Ekland-Olson, and Jonathan R. Sorensen, *The Rope, The Chair, and the Needle: Capital Punishment in Texas, 1923-1990* (Austin: University of Texas Press, 1994), 209.

30   Nat Patton, remarking on the elimination of the poll tax for soldiers said in August 1942, "I don't want to disturb the poll tax, but I don't want to deprive the boys of their chance to vote." Nat Patton quoted in Edward Ryan, "Absences May Kill Soldier Vote Bill," *Washington Post*, August 27, 1942, X5. He later voted against the bill: "Vote to pass H.R. 1024 Which Declares Illegal the Requirement of a Poll Tax as a Prerequisite for Voting or Registering to Vote for President, Vice-President, or U.S. Representative. Oct 13, 1942 (77th Congress)," http://www.govtrack.us/congress/votes/77-1942/h150.

31   Matthias Reiss, "Prisoners Like Us: German POWs and Black Workers on the Fields Felt a Common 'Underdog' Status," *The Atlantic Times*, http://www.atlantic-times.com/archive_detail.php?recordID=1917.

32   Richard Watkins interviewed by Lila Rakoczy, March 21, 2011, in Lila Rakoczy's possession.

33   "Baccus Family Hears From Son in Nazi Prison Camp," *Huntsville Item*, April 12, 1945, 2; "Sgt. R.E. Baccus Freed From Nazis," *Huntsville Item*, July 5, 1945, 1.

34   Cheryl Spencer, "Major Eula Fails Borneman (1908-1986)," *Musings from Sam Houston's Stomping Grounds*; "Lt. Eula Fails, Nurse, Included Among the Missing," *Huntsville Item*, July 29, 1943.

35   Paul A. Neuland, "Field Service Report on Visit to Prisoner of War Camp, Huntsville, Texas, on 17-18 January 1945, by Captain Alexander Lakes," February 7, 1945, RG 389, PMGO, POW Special Projects Division, Administrative Branch Decimal File 1943-46, Box 1615, Camp Haan to Camp Huntsville, MMRB.

Chapter V

1   Nelda Woodall took over the editorial post at the *Huntsville Item* when her husband, Ross Woodall, died on July 7, 1943. "M-Sgt. Ross Woodall given Bronze Star on Italian Front," *Huntsville Item*, May 1, 1945, 1; "PUSHOVER—?," *Huntsville Item*, May 24, 1945, 8.

2   John K. Emmerson, *The Japanese Thread: A Life in the U.S. Foreign Service* (New York: Holt, Rinehart and Winston, 1978), 177-217; John K. Emmerson, "The Indoctrination of Japanese Prisoners of War," April 12, 1945, tab 1 in *Historical Monograph of the Re-Education of Enemy Prisoners of War: Japanese Program*, Office of the Chief of Military History, Historical Section, Office of the Provost Marshal General, Leavenworth, Kansas. On the American decision to place the majority of Japanese POWs with the Commonwealth of Australia, see: Arnold Krammer, "Japanese Prisoners of War in America," *Pacific Historical Review* Vol. 52, No. 1 (Feb., 1983), 70.

3   John Dower, *War Without Mercy: Race and Power in the Pacific War* (New York: Pantheon Books, 1986), 40-41, 45-46.

4   Dower, *War Without Mercy*, 45; Ronald H. Spector, *Eagle Against the Sun: The American War with Japan* (New York: Vintage, 1985), 259-266, 532-540.

5   Dower, *War Without Mercy*, 118-122.

6   Emmerson, *The Japanese Thread*, 177-217; John K. Emmerson, "The Indoctrination of Japanese Prisoners of War," April 12, 1945, tab 1 in *Historical Monograph of the Re-Education of Enemy Prisoners of War: Japanese Program*. Photo to use on Yan'an prisoners: http://collections.lib.uwm.edu/cdm/ref/collection/agsphoto/id/11973.

7   Emmerson, *The Japanese Thread*, 218-219.

8   Ibid., 219.

9   Background information on William B. Gemmill from Edward F. Dunne, Illinois: *The Heart of the Nation, Volume III* (Chicago: Lewis Publishing Company, 1933), 24-26.

10   Biographical information on Charles William Hepner taken from the sketch in his book, *The Kurozumi Sect of Shinto* (reprint Whitefish, MT: Kessinger Publishing, 2007), v-vi. For information on his time as a prisoner in Japan, see: "219 U.S. Civilians Interned in Japan: Official Tokyo List Sent Here Through the Interational Red Cross in Geneva," *New York Times*, March 16, 1942, 7; "3 Missionaries to Be Freed," *New York Times*, June 21, 1942, 32; "Scheduled for Repatriation by the Japanese," *New York Times*, June 25, 1942, 6; Richard C. Wilson, "Interned Writer Finds Food Situation Acute," *Huntingdon (Pennsylvania) Daily News*, July 25, 1942, 1, 10; "Refugees to Sail: Japs' Bullying Bared, Released Internees, Bound for Home, Tell of Cruelty, Suffering While Prisoners," *Oakland Tribune*, July 25, 1942, 1-2.

11   Emmerson, "The Indoctrination of Japanese Prisoners of War," April 12, 1945, tab 1 in *Historical Monograph of the Re-Education of Enemy Prisoners of War: Japanese Program*.

12   Ibid.

13   Ibid.

14   On the historic mis-treatment of Asian immigrants at Angel Island see, Robert Barde and Gustavo J. Bobonis, "Detention at Angle Island: First Empirical Evidence," Social Science History 30:1 (Spring 2006), 103-136; Robert Eric Barde, *Immigration at the Gold Gate: Passenger Ships, Exclusion, and Angel Island* (Westport, CT: Praeger, 2008); Erika Lee and Judy Yung, *Angel Island: Immigrant Gateway to America* (New York: Oxford University Press, 2010), especially chapters 1-3.

15   Charles W. Hepner, "Supplement to Report, 'The Indoctrination of Japanese Prisoners of War,'" tab 2 in *Historical Monograph of the Re-Education of Enemy Prisoners of War: Japanese Program*.

16   Ibid.

17   Peter Edson "Japs Learn Democracy at Unusual Texas Camp" *Milwaukee Journal*, Jan 6, 1946, 46; Justin Williams Sr., "From Charlottesville to Tokyo: Military Government Training and Democratic Reforms in Occupied Japan" *Pacific Historical Review* 51, No. 4 (1982), 414.

18   Boude C. Moore, "Weekly Progress Report, Prisoner of War Camp, Huntsville, Texas," September 29, 1945, RG 389, PMGO, POW Special Projects Division, Administrative Branch Decimal File 1943-46, Box 1615, Camp Haan to Camp Huntsville, MMRB; Boude C. Moore, "Japanese Reorientation Program, Prisoner of War Camp, Huntsville, Texas," October 12, 1945, RG 389, PMGO, POW Special Projects Division, Administrative Branch Decimal File 1943-46, Box 1615, Camp Haan to Camp Huntsville, MMRB.

19   Don MacIver, "Texas Shows Japs Democracy's Ways," *The Dallas Morning News*, December 2, 1945.

20   *Historical Monograph of the Re-Education of Enemy Prisoners of War: Japanese Program*, 34.

21   Boude C. Moore, "Weekly Progress Report, Prisoner of War Camp, Huntsville, Texas," September 11, 1945, RG 389, PMGO, POW Special Projects Division, Administrative Branch Decimal File 1943-46, Box 1615, Camp Haan to Camp Huntsville, MMRB.

22   *Historical Monograph of the Re-Education of Enemy Prisoners of War: Japanese Program*, 8-9.

23   Ibid; Boude C. Moore, Memorandum, "Weekly Progress Report, Prisoner of War Camp, Huntsville, Texas." November 2, 1945, RG 389, PMGO, POW Special Projects Division, Administrative Branch Decimal File 1943-46, Box 1615, Camp Haan to Camp Huntsville, MMRB.

24   *Historical Monograph of the Re-Education of Enemy Prisoners of War: Japanese Program*, 10.

25   Ibid.

26   Boude C. Moore, Memorandum, "Weekly Progress Report, Prisoner of War Camp, Huntsville, Texas," October 26, 1945, RG 389, PMGO, POW Special Projects Division, Administrative Branch Decimal File 1943-46, Box 1615, Camp Haan to Camp Huntsville, MMRB; Boude C. Moore, Memorandum, "Weekly Progress Report, Prisoner of War Camp, Huntsville, Texas," November 2, 1945, RG 389, PMGO, POW Special Projects Division, Administrative Branch Decimal File 1943-46, Box 1615, Camp Haan to Camp Huntsville, MMRB.

27   Marius B. Jansen, *The Making of Modern Japan* (Cambridge: Harvard University Press, 2002), 655.

28   Charles Evans, "Group of 25 Jap Prisoners May Spread Democracy in Homeland," *Houston Chronicle*, December 6, 1945, 1.

29   "Japanese Field Service Code Adopted by the War Department, January 8, 1941," Ibiblio: the Public's Library and Digital Archive, http://ibiblio.org/pha/timeline/410108awp.html.

30   John W. Dower, *Embracing Defeat: Japan in the Wake of World War II* (New York: W.W. Norton & Company, 1999), 277.

31   "Japanese Field Service Code," Section 4: Unity, Ibiblio: the Public's Library and Digital Archive, http://ibiblio.org/pha/timeline/410108awp.html.

32   Jansen, *Making of Modern Japan*, 655.

33   *Historic Monograph of the Re-education of Enemy Prisoners of War, Japanese Program*, 22, 13, 14.

34   "Local Opinions on Surrender Are Divided," *Huntsville Item*, August 16, 1945, 1.

35   Yamaga Moriji was "one of the Japanese navy's top meteorological experts, who, in this capacity, provided the Allies considerable information on Japanese and Russian capabilities. His interrogators also learned that, while some four hundred fifty Japanese crypt-analysts encountered great difficulty in attempts to break the codes of the Western Allies, they succeeded in breaking Soviet weather codes," in Ulrich Straus, *The Anguish of Surrender: Japanese POWs of World War II* (Seattle: University of Washington Press, 2003), 261, note 4.

36   *Historical Monograph of the Re-Education of Enemy Prisoners of War: Japanese Program*, 14.

37   Ibid, 14-15.

38   Ibid., 15.

39   Ibid., 16.

40   Ibid, 18.

41   Edward Davison, "Relaxation of Certain Prisoner of War Regulations," September 21, 1945, RG 389, PMGO, POW Special Projects Division, Administrative Branch Decimal File 1943-46, Box 1615, Camp Haan to Camp Huntsville, MMRB.

42   Boude C. Moore, "Weekly Progress Report, Prisoner of War Camp, Huntsville, Texas," October 19, 1945, RG 389, PMGO, POW Special Projects

Division, Administrative Branch Decimal File 1943-46, Box 1615, Camp Haan to Camp Huntsville, MMRB.

43   Ibid.

44   William A. McIlwaine, "Weekly Progress Report," December 14, 1945, RG 389, PMGO, POW Special Projects Division, Administrative Branch Decimal File 1943-46, Box 1615, Camp Haan to Camp Huntsville, MMRB.

45   H.E. Thompson, "Prisoner of War Camp Labor Report," September 30, 1945 to December 31, 1945, RG 389, PMGO, POW Special Projects Division, Camps Inactivated - 8th Service Command, Gueydan to Lockport, Reporting Branch Subject File 1942-46, Enemy POW Information Bureau, Box 2507, MMRB; *Historical Monograph of the Re-Education of Enemy Prisoners of War: Japanese Program*, 17.

46   Ibid.

47   *Historical Monograph of the Re-Education of Enemy Prisoners of War: Japanese Program*, 9

48   Ibid., 19.

49   C.W. Hepner, "Project Progress Report," October 12, 1945, Box 1615, RG 389, PMGO, POW Special Projects Division, Administrative Branch Decimal File 1943-46, Box 1615, Camp Haan to Camp Huntsville, MMRB.

Chapter VI

1   Ty Cashion, *Sam Houston State University, An Institutional Memory 1879-2004* (Huntsville, Texas: Texas Review Press, 2004), 96; "Vet Plea For Rent Control Answered by Rep. Pickett," *Houstonian*, September 20, 1946, 1; Alice P. Lakavage, *Houstonian*, December 13, 1984, 1.

2   Frances Handley Bowers, "History of the Country Campus," (Master's Thesis, Sam Houston State Teachers College, 1950), 30.

3   John C. Bowie to President Harmon, November 14, 1956 and Lowman and Harmon Lowman to John C. Bowie, November 16, 1956, Country Campus Vertical Files, Thomason Special Collections Room, Newton Gresham Library, Sam Houston State University.

4   John Meritt, "Twice Over Lightly," *Houstonian*, October 17, 1946, 1.

5   Sam Houston State Teachers College. Bulletin. 1946-1947, Thomason Special Collections Room, Newton Gresham Library, Sam Houston State University.

6   Bowers, "History of the Country Campus," 46.

7   Lakavage, *Houstonian*, December 13, 1984, 1.

8   "Faculty Makes Homes of Country Campus Buildings, *Houstonian*, November 8, 1946, 1.

9   "Fifty-Six Couples Reside at C.C.," *Houstonian*, October 11, 1946, 1.

10   "98 Construction Men At Work on The Apartments," *Houstonian*, February 7, 1947, 1.

11   *The Country Campus Journal*, July 1, 1948, Thomason Special Collections Room, Newton Gresham Library, Sam Houston State University.

12   Josey School 1947-48 vertical file, Thomason Special Collections Room, Newton Gresham Library, Sam Houston State University; *The Country Campus Journal*, October 9, 1948, Thomason Special Collections Room, Newton Gresham Library, Sam Houston State University.

13   Vicki Kelly, *Houstonian*, March 21, 1975, 5; Frieda Koeninger interviewed by Carolyn Carroll, October 4, 2011, in Carolyn Carroll's possession; "C C Veterans Organize Legion Post," *Houstonian*, November 8, 1946; *Houstonian*, December 20, 1946.

14   *The Country Campus Journal*, July 1, 1948-August 13, 1948, Thomason Special Collections Room, Newton Gresham Library, Sam Houston State University.

15   "Students to Vote," *Houstonian*, November 11, 1950.

16   "County Campus Chatter," *Huntsville Item*, December 28, 1950.

17   "CC Chapter of FFA Chooses to Remain as Separate Chapter," *Houstonian*, September 30, 1950.

18   Lakavage, *Houstonian*, December 13, 1984, 1.

19   "L S Baseball Camp In Final Session," *Houstonian*, July 25, 1952.

20   "Baseball Scholarship Camp will Begin Monday at C.C.," *Houstonian*, June 15, 1957.

21   "C.C. Training Plans Not Set According to Pirate Big-Wigs," *Houstonian*, January 8, 1955; "Pirate Come—Lowman Added Rub-down hose for the Pitchers," *Houstonian*, March 5, 1955.

22   "Bigger CC Planned for 1000 Students," *Houstonian*, May 2, 1947.

23   Josey School Bulletin, 1951-1952, Thomason Room, Newton Gresham Library, Sam Houston State University.

24   "20 Students in Vocational Courses," *Houstonian*, October 25, 1952.

25   Harmon Lowman to Agnes Brown, July 19, 1948, Josey School 1947-1948 vertical file, Thomason Special Collections Room, Newton Gresham Library, Sam Houston State University; Josey School Bulletin, 1951-1952. Thomason Special Collections Room, Newton Gresham Library, Sam Houston State University.

26   *Houstonian*, November 1, 1952; "College Students To Build Girl Scout 'Little House,'" *Huntsville Item*, January 18, 1951; Josey Student Builds Tractor," *Houstonian*, May 9, 1951.

27   "Pasture Program Discussed," *Houstonian*, March 21, 1951; "C.C. Residents Work on Gardens," *Houstonian*, April 21, 1951; Board of Regents Minutes, June 11, 1953, Thomason Special Collections Room, Newton Gresham Library, Sam Houston State University; "School Farm Pays Way of Students," *Houstonian*, December 6, 1952; "Fire victims New Homes," *Houstonian*, April 11, 1951.

28   Sam Houston State Teacher's College Bulletin, Daily Schedule of Classes, 1948-49, 1950-51, 1951-1952, Thomason Special Collections Room, Newton Gresham Library, Sam Houston State University.

29   "Enrollment Falls Below Par at 1165," *Houstonian*, June 20, 1952; "Regent Views Two-Fold Plan of College," *Houstonian*, June 22, 1951; "Board of Regents Approved College's Decrease Budget," *Houstonian*, August 10, 1951; "Enrollment Figure Climbs to 1,285," *Houstonian*, September 20, 1952.

30   "Country Campus Future Development to Cost $32 million Proposed by SHSTC," *Huntsville Item*, Country Campus vertical files, Thomason Special Collections Room, Newton Gresham Library, Sam Houston State University; "Twenty-Year Plan for SHSTC," President's Report to the Board of Regents, 1956, Country Campus vertical files, Thomason Special Collections Room, Newton Gresham Library, Sam Houston State University.

31   "Cleanup Campaign For County Campus Notes History of Facility," *Huntsville Item*, June 24, 1971.

32   "Star Gazing Captivates Astronomy Instructor," *Houstonian*, July 20, 1993.

33   Board of Regents Minutes, December 4-5, 1997, Thomason Special Collections Room, Newton Gresham Library, Sam Houston State University.

34   "New Observatory Under Construction," Physics Department, Sam
      Houston State University.

35   Dedication Brochure, Country Campus vertical files, Thomason Special
      Collections Room, Newton Gresham Library, Sam Houston State University.